# THE TROUBLE WITH HISTORY

# THE
# TROUBLE
# WITH
# HISTORY

Morality, Revolution, and Counterrevolution

## ADAM MICHNIK

Edited by Irena Grudzinska Gross

Translated by

Elzbieta Matynia, Agnieszka Marczyk, and Roman Czarny

Foreword by James Davison Hunter and John M. Owen IV

Yale UNIVERSITY PRESS/NEW HAVEN & LONDON

Published with the assistance of the Institute for Advanced Studies in
Culture, University of Virginia.

Yale University Press books may be purchased in quantity for
educational, business, or promotional use. For information, please e-mail
sales.press@yale.edu (U.S. office) or sales@yaleup.co.uk (U.K. office).

Designed by Mary Valencia.
Set in Caslon type by IDS Infotech Ltd.
Printed in the United States of America.

*Library of Congress Cataloging-in-Publication Data*
Michnik, Adam.
The trouble with history : morality, revolution, and counterrevolution /
Adam Michnik ; edited by Irena Grudzinska Gross ; translated by
Elzbieta Matynia, Agnieszka Marczyk, and Roman Czarny.
pages      cm — (Politics and culture)
Includes bibliographical references and index.
ISBN 978-0-300-18597-3 (alk. paper)

1. Democracy—Moral and ethical aspects. 2. Political ethics. 3. Post-
communism—Poland. 4. Poland—Politics and government—1989–
5. Jacobins. 6. France—Politics and government—1789–1799.
I. Grudzinska-Gross, Irena, editor. II. Title.
JC423.M5958 2014
172'.1—dc23         2013037728
A catalogue record for this book is available from the British Library.

# CONTENTS

More than and prior to a political system, liberal democracy is a public culture defined by a set of practices and norms for public engagement, an engagement that centers around a cluster of ideals and propositions about liberty, justice, and the common good. Such ideals are vital because even in the highly fluid and fragmented circumstances of the modern and late modern period, they define the public and political terms of human flourishing. Notwithstanding its flaws and susceptibility to corruption, liberal democracy is recognized the world over as the public manifestation of the common good; as Tomáš Masaryk put it, "the political form of the humane ideal." This is why regimes everywhere—even the most thuggish, authoritarian, and anti-democratic—want to be thought of as democratic. Even when denied in practice, the word provides a mantle of legitimacy to those who exercise power in its name.

It is for this reason that contemporary democratic politics can never be understood as *only* about the interests and actions of political economy or power alone. The moral and ethical dimension of modern democratic politics is intrinsic: not only impossible to disentangle from the actual actions and procedures of the state, but foundational to any government that calls itself democratic. Freedom, tolerance, hope, and respect for human dignity are not secondary, then, but primary. As we witness among democratic revolutionaries everywhere, they matter absolutely. Such ideals have made it possible to endure not only the indignities and suffering imposed by oppressive powers but also, often enough, the world's indifference to their struggle.

The conditions that make for vibrant democracies are fragile; all the more so in populations divided by wealth, race, ethnicity, religion, language, and tribe. Whatever else might be entailed, they require some minimal understandings of justice that are shared and binding across all differences. This is the foundation of any legitimacy a regime can hope for. But those understandings also have to be credibly and consistently approximated within its political institutions and practices. Without those shared commitments and credible enactments, constitutions will become hollow speech acts, emptied of authority and, in the end, a "parchment barrier" to tyranny. Democracy may retain certain formality, but the authority that underwrites it loses its humanizing constraints, leaving a political machinery capable of the crudest expressions of domination on behalf of some factional interests against others.

Even now, late into modernity, religion would seem to make matters more combustible. While religious faith can have an important salubrious effect in the cultivation of civic virtue and social capital, certain forms of politically assertive religion are clearly sources of social antagonism, foes of democratic freedom, and perpetrators of grotesque human injustice, not least when they claim the label of democracy. At the same time, it is apparent that the will to meaning takes expression in ultimate beliefs no less sacred by being naturalistic and non-theistic, no less authoritarian and oppressive by being non-religious. And so it is that secular ideologies can be every bit as hostile to freedom and justice in a pluralistic society as religious orthodoxies—here too under the aegis of high-minded principle. The abiding temptation, as regimes come and go, is for one type of authoritarianism to replace another. Indeed, as John Milton observed a century after the Reformation, "new Presbyter is old Priest writ large." The abuse of power in the name of virtue, the corruption of virtue through the violence of lies, but also the power of truth and desire for freedom are common factors in the dynamics of modern political history.

There is, then, much that is murky in the interplay of morality and politics, but also much that is at stake. What is most obviously at stake is democracy itself—a democracy that meaningfully lives up to its name. Modern liberal democracy was anchored in certain moral possibilities and its legitimacy was always and invariably tied to its realization in political practice. Do these possibilities continue to carry any moral authority? There is no question of their psychological appeal, but what are the cultural sources that might make them compelling, even authoritative guides for ordering a peaceable, even if contentious, pluralism? These questions could seem merely academic except that they contain within them what is at stake for actual people and their communities.

In the early decades of the twenty-first century, liberal democracies—those that are well established and those that are emerging—are suffering from various crises of legitimacy, as publics are given many reasons to distrust those who govern them and the rules and authority by which they govern. Needless to say, crises of legitimacy are hardly new, yet in our own day, they play out in historically unique settings with historically distinctive effect. On the ground, these play out differently, in different degrees, and in different places, but not least in some of the strongest democracies in the world today. Publics are deeply pessimistic about the actual state of their governing institutions, often disaffected from the large-scale political establishments that order their collective lives, and regularly cynical toward their political leadership in their claims to deliver on their promises.

The Institute for Advanced Studies in Culture and Yale University Press are launching an exploration of these themes in a series examining democracy and its discontents. What are the complex factors that are challenging and transforming the normative foundations of democracy and the democratic impulse in the late modern world? In the case of established modern democracies, can this Enlightenment-era institution survive in an increasingly post-Enlightenment culture? If so, how and on what terms? In the case of emerging democracies, what cultural endowments will underwrite liberal democratic institutions and practices against the temptations of authoritarianism in its various expressions?

These broad meta-questions find historical expression in particular settings—national and global. In these different settings, they take shape both in the changing contours of pluralism and in the changing dynamics of cultural solidarity, all magnified by the paradoxical force of religion. While reflecting a certain breadth in empirical focus, this series will pursue the common theme of exploring the changing normative dynamics that underwrite modern and emerging democracies and global democratic institutions—how these dynamics strengthen, weaken, threaten, or inhibit the realization of liberal democratic ideals in the late modern world.

There could be no way to better anchor this series than with Adam Michnik's book *The Trouble with History*. Michnik, one of the founding fathers of Polish democracy and a man of extraordinary moral courage, has been a witness to and participant in these political, cultural, and ethical dynamics at the end of the Soviet rule and the years following. His reflections on politics and morality in the French Revolution and in pre- and post-Communist Poland provide poignant and powerful lessons on the struggles of creating a meaningful democratic rule and the fragility of sustaining it. They are lessons that speak far beyond Poland to emerging and established democracies everywhere.

James Davison Hunter and
John M. Owen IV, Series Editors

PART ONE

# ONE

# Morality in Politics:
# Willy Brandt's Two Trips to Poland

It was a very difficult journey: in December 1970, Willy Brandt, the chancellor of the Federal Republic of Germany (commonly known as West Germany), came to Warsaw to sign an agreement recognizing the Polish-German border along the Oder-Neisse line. After signing the document, he laid flowers at the Tomb of the Unknown Soldier and then went to the Ghetto Heroes Monument. He laid a wreath there as well. He straightened both ends of the wreath and stepped back on the wet granite. For a moment he was motionless. And then he fell to his knees, his head bowed.

Brandt did not prearrange this gesture with anyone on either the Polish or the German side. He always said that he did what people do when words fail. In this way, he honored the memory of millions of those who were murdered. It was commented then that he "knelt to give expression to his remorse, remorse for heinous deeds done in the name of Germany, thereby taking the guilt upon his own shoulders, though he did not in fact bear the guilt himself."[1] This gesture, according to Brandt's biographer Peter Merseburger, showed him as a politician who establishes moral criteria that reach far beyond his country.[2]

Brandt's moral criteria could be shocking for the politicians of the Western world. For us, Central and Eastern European dissidents, they were self-evident. Our political engagement did not arise out of struggle for power but out of struggle for freedom. Politics was for us, as for Brandt—an antifascist and ex-émigré—not a means of realizing the interests of specific social groups, but a struggle to rescue values. It therefore demanded— to use Aristotle's language—"moral courage."

Yet the moral courage of the dissident world changed its form in the world of real politics. This was at times surprising and painful for the dissidents. Real politics forced these uncompromising people to make a series of compromises between what they wanted to do and what they could do, between the voice of conscience and the pragmatic dictate of common sense.

When he came to Warsaw in December 1970, Willy Brandt was guided by political pragmatics. He sought to finalize German reparations for Nazism in the international arena. At the same time, the new *Ostpolitik* was to bring the Federal Republic out of self-isolation and make Germany a fully independent political actor on the European scene.

The formal recognition of the Oder-Neisse line aroused many critical voices on the German right, especially among the "expellees," former inhabitants of German territories annexed to Poland after the war. It was stubbornly repeated that one cannot relinquish old German lands in the east. One of the newspapers claimed that Brandt threw away the East Germans' right to self-determination and to their fatherland. In his replies Brandt pointed out that the agreement with Poland did not sacrifice anything that had not already been long lost—not by the government of the Federal Republic but by the "criminal National Socialist regime."

The new *Ostpolitik* was full of traps, but Brandt believed that it was realistic and morally indispensable. He said that words like Auschwitz will long accompany both Polish and German nations and remind them that hell on earth is possible. One should think of the future and recognize morality as a political force.

The photograph of Brandt kneeling before the Ghetto Heroes Monument made its way around the world and changed the image of both Germany and the German chancellor. It was only in Poland that it was never published—except in one Jewish paper which nobody read. At that time in Poland Jews were spoken of badly or not at all. In the eyes of anti-Semitic Polish nationalists he knelt in front of the wrong monument.

A young Polish sociologist, born a decade after Brandt's gesture, recently wrote—certainly without bad intentions—that even though it took place in Poland, Brandt's gesture was clearly addressed not to Poles but to Jews. I can only juxtapose my own memories against this: I took Brandt's gesture as an homage paid to all victims of Nazism, victims from all nations, although the choice of the Ghetto Heroes Monument was obvious—Jews suffered the most. At the same time, it was a slap in the face, very precisely aimed, at the anti-Semites from the communist government. By censoring the photograph of the kneeling Brandt from the papers, they unknowingly signaled that they correctly read the gesture of the chancellor and antifascist. During that time, I thought about Brandt often and with affection.

I thought: here is a man who risked his life in the conspiracy against Hitler. Here is a man who stood up against his own nation when this nation chose Hitler in elections; a man accused by nationalists of national treason because he worked for the anti-Hitler coalition. Today this man is a chancellor and he is extending his hand to Poles and to Poland. (I had a chance to say this to Brandt in person in Hamburg, in the fall of 1989.)

I

In Germany, commentators wrote that "Brandt the moralist" divided the nation. Public opinion polls said 41 percent of respondents believed that his "kneeling" was appropriate while 48 percent thought it was overdone. The older generation evaluated Brandt's gesture negatively, but, as Brandt's biographer points out, for younger Germans the image of the kneeling Brandt etched itself in their memory as a symbol of morality in politics, which they felt was lacking. No polls were conducted in Poland.

Shortly after Brandt's visit, strikes broke out in Gdansk and other coastal cities. For the communist leader of Poland, Władysław Gomułka, his greatest political success—the acceptance of the Oder-Neisse border by the Federal Republic—coincided with his spectacular defeat: the rebellion of the workers swept him off the political scene forever. This does not change the fact that the success of Gomułka and his regime was self-evident. But we—the dissidents against this regime—also had our success. The agreement with the Federal Republic neutralized the most dangerous of the arguments used in the propaganda of "People's Poland": namely, that Poles should obey the government because Germans were waiting in ambush to attack Poland again and take back the western lands.

Memory of Nazi atrocities was vivid and constantly fueled. So this anti-German gun was always loaded. It proved effective in 1966 during the smear campaign organized after the Polish bishops' letter to the German bishops. It was fired once again in August 1968 in order to justify, in the eyes of many, the intervention of Warsaw Pact armies in Czechoslovakia as a way of preempting German encroachment there. In December 1970, this gun was useless—the shipyard workers from

Gdansk and Szczecin were not accused of acting on behalf of West German revanchists.

Brandt was joined by a group of eminent German intellectuals, including Günter Grass. Grass, in turn, in his interviews for the Polish press, respectfully mentioned Polish writers, like Leszek Kołakowski and Sławomir Mrożek, who were censured after 1968. He also fondly recalled émigré writers. For me, this was a signal that Brandt's *Ostpolitik* was directed not only against the ruling communists, but also toward the society that was standing up to the dictatorship.

## II

Günter Grass and Brandt were friends. In 1969, during the electoral campaign leading up to the success of the Social Democratic Party (SPD) and Brandt's term as chancellor, Grass was afraid that, if Brandt were to win, he would become an object of hate. Years later, Grass reconstructed a monologue of a hateful reporter, a monologue about the kneeling chancellor:

"It looks like the same old routine . . . but no, he's got something up his sleeve: down he goes, down on the wet granite, with no support from his hands, no, he clasps his hands in front of his balls and puts a holier-than-the

Pope look on his face, holds out for a good minute or so till the shutters stop clicking, then picks himself up, but not the easy way, first one foot, then the other, no, in one go—he must've practiced it for days in front of the mirror—and then he stands there as if he'd just seen the Holy Ghost, as if to show the Poles, no, the whole world—how photogenic eating humble pie can be."[3]

The hateful reporter cannot stand that "a man who fought in a Norwegian uniform against us, against Germans, has come here with his retinue . . . to hand our Pomerania, Silesia, and East Prussia to the Poles on a platter, and then does his knee-bend number for them to boot. . . . He makes my blood boil. . . . When I saw him kneeling there in the rain . . . It was revolting. . . . I hate the guy's guts."[4]

On various occasions, Brandt was accused of being a British, American, or Soviet agent, a crypto-communist, a crypto-Trotskyite, a cold-war revanchist, and a capitulator before the Soviet Union, as well as an alcoholic born out of wedlock. Insinuations, slander, hatred, and intrigue—all this accompanied him throughout his life.

Brandt, a young socialist, was deeply affected by the defeat of German social democracy in 1933. He belonged to the generation of the lost, homeless Left, which saw fascism as a product of capitalist economy, and believed that only a socialist revolution would be an effective prescription against it. This way of thinking was accompanied by the conviction that socialists and communists should form a united front against fascism. Yet communism, through its practice—the Moscow trials and the exploits of the Soviet security services during the Spanish Civil War—made this hope a hopeless pipe dream. Then he witnessed the Ribbentrop-Molotov Pact. He saw it as treason of the workers' movement, and he saw the USSR—a country where capitalism had been eliminated—as a state ruled by terror, oppression, and tyranny.

Later—despite his own hesitation—he confirmed this conviction when he observed the Sovietization of East Germany (the German Democratic Republic), the blockade of West Berlin, the uprising of Berlin workers (1953), the Hungarian uprising (1956), and the construction of the Berlin Wall (1961).

III

Konrad Adenauer, the leader of the Christian Democrats and the first chancellor of the Federal Republic, viewed Stalin without illusions. Starting in 1940, Adenauer claimed, Stalin carried out a consistent policy of subordinating successive countries, whether by annexation or by creating satellite states. This was also the meaning of Stalin's policies aimed at Germany—first, he wanted to remove American troops from Germany and Europe, so that he could later gain control over Germany by means of "neutralizing" the united German state.

To prevent this, Adenauer strove to integrate West Germany into the structures of the Western world. He did not believe in making agreements with Stalin regarding German unification because, at that time, such unification could have been possible only under Soviet hegemony. As a consequence of this reasoning, Adenauer denied legitimacy to the German Democratic Republic (GDR), an artificial creation of Soviet politics. This included the refusal to recognize the Polish-German border along the Oder-Neisse line. Adenauer stubbornly repeated that "the country on the other side of the Oder and Neisse rivers belongs to us, to Germany." At that time leaders of the SPD often voiced similar opinions.

Adenauer thought Stalin had a scenario for Germany analogous to the one he observed in the Korean War. The East German government would join the effort to "liberate the people of the Federal Republic," the United States would remain passive in the face of a German civil war, while "the population of the Federal Republic would remain neutral toward the invading army from the Soviet sector—for psychological reasons, since this army would consist of Germans." After Stalin's death, this political logic was subject to only slight modifications.

At the same time, Adenauer's politics led to rebuilding the economy, stabilization of the institutions of parliamentary democracy, and overcoming the post-Nazi trauma. Adenauer repeated that the subject of "German guilt" must be closed; that "one can no longer differentiate between two classes of people in Germany: those politically blameless and those burdened with responsibility." The success of his politics was indisputable—the German economy was experiencing its "miracle," the Federal Republic reached full sovereignty and became a respected member of the Atlantic community.

Adenauer's policies directed at the GDR were also effective: the Federal Republic was winning the rivalry between the two systems, and East Germans were leaving the "state of workers and peasants" en masse to live in the world of "rotting capitalism." As head of the communist government, Walter Ulbricht alarmed Moscow by warning that if the policy of open borders was not changed, East Germany's collapse was inevitable.

In response to this, the Soviets constructed the Berlin Wall. This was an obvious defeat of Soviet socialism on German soil. What is significant, however, is that it was also a defeat for Adenauer's politics, of the complete boycott of all Soviet bloc states except the USSR. The Americans (and other Western nations) limited themselves to verbal declarations. In the clash with aggressive Soviet power, no one wanted to die for Berlin.

Willy Brandt, the mayor of West Berlin, had to draw his conclusions from this. He observed the helplessness of German politics, imprisoned in the dogmas of anti-communist "indomitability." He understood that no war would return Germany to its prewar borders, that the West would not support any anti-Soviet revolutions, just as it did nothing for Berlin workers in 1953 or the rebelling Hungarians in 1956. This gave birth to his new *Ostpolitik*—if the "iron curtain" could not be knocked down, it had to be made permeable. Such was Brandt's political idea.

IV

*Ostpolitik* was to be an art of realizing concrete goals, such as, for example, the rights of the inhabitants of both sides of Berlin to contact one another; but it was also to open possibilities for more distant goals, which looked to the future to discern the outlines of utopia. Brandt wanted to open the way to a German-German dialogue, to a rapprochement, even to some form of German unity.

Already in 1963 he clearly formulated the meaning of *Ostpolitik*. The German problem, for him, could be solved only with the Soviet Union and not against it. This required time, but it would not seem so long if the lives of Germans on the other side of the Wall, and communication with them, could be made easier. And *Ostpolitik* had its successes. Agreements with East Berlin indeed made contacts between members of separated families and visits in both parts of Germany easier; they also enabled the Federal Republic to ransom political prisoners. The price of this was the gradual legitimization of the communist dictatorship in East Germany. And arguments about the limits of this legitimization were emerging.

It seems that the effects of *Ostpolitik* were ambiguous. Brandt was certainly able to maintain Germany's Adenauerian European and Atlantic orientation, while also enriching it with new and original policy toward the East. West Germany became a "normal" European state, breaking out of its self-isolation. But—at what price?

## V

Brandt's *Ostpolitik* converged with Richard Nixon and Henry Kissinger's policy of détente. Still, American leaders did not fully trust Brandt; they suspected that his flirtation with Leonid Brezhnev could mean that the cost of unification would be the Finlandization and neutralization of Germany.

Was there reason for such concerns? Brandt's biographer has described the chancellor's informal meeting with Brezhnev in Crimea in September 1971, when—in the course of sixteen hours of intensive talks—they developed trust and personal liking. Brandt's biographer wrote that there was "chemistry" between them, that they both loved wine, women, and carousing, that both told jokes and laughed readily.

This nice image of Brandt and Brezhnev's friendship was to obscure reality. People were suffering in Soviet gulags and dying from bullets when they tried to cross from East to West Berlin. This provoked sharp criticism of Brandt and his politics. Rainer Barzel, a leader of the Christian Democrats, announced, for example, that he would not have signed the agreement with the GDR unless the East Germans immediately agreed to stop shooting at escapees. Brandt nonetheless saw the continuation of the politics of rapprochement—described as "the maintenance of peace"—as an overriding goal.

The politics of consistent rapprochement with Moscow and East Berlin and the language of "concern for peace" practically drove out concern for human rights in Central and Eastern Europe. Helmut Schmidt, who followed Brandt as chancellor, saw the human rights campaign led by Jimmy Carter and Zbigniew Brzezinski as "naïve, and even dangerous." Schmidt, as leader of the SPD, and other politicians from his party said much about ending the arms race, but not a word about liberation movements in Warsaw Pact countries. Violations of human rights in Latin America or South Africa were stigmatized; repressions in the USSR, Poland, Romania, or Czechoslovakia were passed over in silence.

In talks with East Berlin, the issue of repressions against dissidents was not broached, unless the conversation turned to the ransom of prisoners; as if they were hostages held by gangster hijackers. Heinrich August Winkler, an excellent historian who is close to the SPD, claimed that during his visits to the capitals of communist countries, when it came to cases of severe persecution, Willy Brandt followed the principle of intervening only in private conversations, avoiding any gestures of solidarity with the advocates of human rights.

VI

The SPD's attitude toward the Solidarity trade union movement and martial law in Poland, imposed in December 1981, was a typical example of this stance. The SPD political philosophy assumed that democratic change in the Soviet bloc was possible only if it did not unsettle the ruling elites. Stabilization was a condition of reform; changes were possible only when carried out in collaboration with the elites, not against them. Only "top-down" reform, carried out with Moscow's permission, was possible. Viewed from this perspective, Solidarity was disrupting the détente process in Europe. SPD leaders said that if "in the name of preserving peace" Germans were not insisting on the idea of unification, and GDR citizens were enduring the Soviet diktat without protest, then Poles, too, should restrain their aspirations to freedom. Winkler claimed that SPD's sympathy toward Solidarity was limited, above all, by the fact that this trade union was not leftist and socialist, but national and Catholic. In 1981, according to him, Solidarity was increasingly seen as a destructive factor, bringing chaos to Poland and endangering Europe's stabilization, or even world peace. Because Germany was divided, the ensuing worsening of East-West relations was most detrimental for the Federal Republic.

On December 11, 1981, Chancellor Helmut Schmidt began an official visit in the GDR. On December 13, Schmidt and the East German leader Erich Honecker were caught by surprise at news of the introduction of martial law in Poland. Schmidt came up with a brief declaration: "Mr. Honecker, like myself, is shocked by the fact that what happened was nonetheless necessary."[5] On December 18, Willy Brandt, by this time chairman of the Socialist International, declared that the Polish government was not interrupting the process of reform and renewal of the country, but rather desired to continue this process. This aroused angry protests from Bettino Craxi, head of the Italian Socialist Party, and French president François Mitterrand. The International soon issued a statement stigmatizing the repressions and calling for a resumption of the politics of dialogue. Brandt saw this as a politics of empty gestures. He believed that, by introducing martial law, Premier Wojciech Jaruzelski, "a Polish patriot to the marrow," had saved Poland from Soviet intervention.

A specifically German factor was at work as well. In an interview with *Die Zeit*, Brandt explained that as a German he could not talk about camps in Poland, where dissidents and worker activists were imprisoned, because this would provoke questions about the other camps that had once existed on Poland's territory. When he accepted the Oder-Neisse border in the name of the Federal Republic, Brandt had spoken to all Poles. Later he spoke only to Poland's communist governing elite.

## VII

In December 1985, Brandt came to Poland at the government's invitation to participate in the fifteenth anniversary of the signing of the Warsaw Pact. It was a sad visit; its only result was another gesture of legitimization of the regime of generals and party secretaries, who were still imprisoning and repressing the people of Solidarity.

When he visited South Africa, Brandt met with Winnie Mandela and made a public request to meet with the imprisoned Nelson Mandela. The request was rejected, but the gesture of solidarity remained. During his visit in Poland, he did not make any gestures toward Solidarity activists who were fighting for freedom, though we, and I personally, asked for it. Timothy Garton Ash wrote that, because Brandt was "the very symbol of German-Polish reconciliation," Solidarity activists were dismayed when "he shook the hands of the Generals and Party Secretaries. He spoke of reconciliation, peace, normalization, stability. But he visited no prisons . . . , laid no flowers on the murdered workers' graves—nor on that of the martyred Father Popiełuszko. He declined an invitation to meet his fellow Nobel Peace Prize winner, Lech Walesa, in Solidarity's capital, Gdansk."[6] His biographer wondered if Brandt, the Nobel laureate, saw in Walesa a fundamentalist Catholic reactionary, and whether he was afraid of an explosion of new nationalisms in the Eastern bloc. Perhaps Solidarity was too spontaneous a movement for him?

His behavior during his visit was taken by Solidarity as a slap in the face.

The dispute about martial law has divided Poland for thirty years. My generation never accepted the awful logic of martial law, the long years of forfeited opportunities. Today I try to understand General Jaruzelski's motivations from that time, which, of course, does not mean that I share his point of view. I nonetheless think—and I already believed in 1982—that martial law was decidedly a lesser evil than a possible Soviet intervention. Remembering Hungary in 1956 or Czechoslovakia in 1968, I cannot rule out the possibility that intervention would have been unavoidable.

I can understand the ambivalence in Brandt's and the SPD's reactions after December 13, 1981. The caution of these reactions was probably an expression of helplessness or of relief that Soviet intervention did not take place. The years that followed, however, were a time not of reform but of stagnation and repressions. At that time, Soviet intervention no longer threatened Poland. Vaclav Havel wrote about "the power of the powerless"; Willy Brandt demonstrated the moral powerlessness of the powerful.

VIII

Brandt was a visionary who believed in common sense. He stood by this as the mayor of West Berlin and as the leader of the SPD. He was not naive, but he was also not cynical. He understood his own powerlessness when Berlin was divided by a wall and barbed wire. He was able to control an enraged crowd, but at the same time he was also able to call things by their true name: he spoke about the "walls of a concentration camp," which were a lethal blow to the city and which would become "prison walls for the entire nation."

He was a politician of passion who dreamed of a Germany that would shake off the burden of the Nazi past and the domination of Soviet garrisons over the GDR. He knew, however, that changes have to take place gradually, in small steps (Grass called this the snail's philosophy). He knew that no actual order could be ideal, and the duty of the politician was to uphold human rights, to embrace the philosophy of reconciling various interests, and to maintain balance.

He must have looked with disgust at the corruption rampant in the world of parliamentary politics; he was repulsed by the dirty wave of deception, which his adversaries did not spare him. He had to accept it, however, if he desired to realize the most important—also in a moral sense—aims of his politics. Still—I believe— there was a certain price he did not have to pay.

IX

The idea of "change through rapprochement" was transformed into the philosophy of "rapprochement through fraternization"—one can get this sense when one follows the "joint struggle for peace" carried out by Brandt and Brezhnev or by the leaders of the SPD and the GDR. Brandt's attitude was marked by loyalty to the German *Ostpolitik*, and by empathy for the makers of martial law. He had no empathy whatsoever for the victims of martial law. Imprisoned by the generals, they were additionally sentenced to oblivion by the Western world. Geopolitics drove out morality.

When confronted with this, the defenders of *Ostpolitik* say that peace was the greatest moral value for them. It does not seem likely, however, that denouncing the martial law regime with the same rhetoric as that directed against dictatorships in other parts of the world would have been a threat to world peace. The harsh language of President Reagan or the French Socialists did not trigger war. A gesture of solidarity with political prisoners would not have been an act of cold-war belligerence, but an act of loyalty to one's own biography and one's own—so frequently declared—system of ethical values.

The SPD leaders claimed that one cannot place ideology on the same plane as the preservation of peace and use human rights to destabilize the political situation. This was the essence of the great mistake of "transformation through rapprochement": Brandt, a Nobel laureate, disregarded the obvious requirement that the politics of détente and peace should not ignore the difference between democracy and freedom and communist dictatorship—and that it should also not ignore the victims of this dictatorship.

This was not the only mistake. The loss of a clear image of communist dictatorship was another one. In the Brezhnev era it was no longer a system of Stalinist totalitarian oppression, but it retained the institutions of a totalitarian state. For their part, the leaders of the SPD stubbornly repeated that the time of ideology had passed, and a time of interests was at hand. In the summer of 1981, Brandt spoke about Brezhnev and the leaders of the Communist Party of the Soviet Union:

"They want to negotiate. And regarding Brezhnev, one can say whatever one will, but he is deeply concerned about world peace." One could see how much Brezhnev wanted to negotiate by following the Polish-Soviet negotiations in 1981; one could see how deeply he cared for peace by taking a cursory look at the war in Afghanistan.

After many years, Klaus Bölling, the press secretary of Helmut Schmidt's government, recalled Schmidt's meeting with Honecker in December 1981. He wrote that it was only then that some members of the government realized how futile was the hope that they could get the leaders of the GDR to agree with their position. Bölling accurately identified the mistake of the SPD leaders as self-deception. An hour-long conversation, or a reading of the speeches of leaders of the GDR, was sufficient to realize their narrow-mindedness, and their fanatical intolerance toward those with other ideas and ways of life. They condemned books they had not read, people they did not try to understand, a world they mortally feared.

The leaders of the SPD knew what communist enslavement was, but they did not understand the mentality of the Soviet leaders. They believed that they were "reasonable" rulers, but their rationality operated within a framework of a different, "non-Western" mentality. The framework of this rationality teemed with motivations that went beyond the mental horizon of the Social Democrats, who understood neither the invasion of Afghanistan nor the permanent Stasi surveillance of Brandt.

X

According to many opinions, Reagan's hard-line politics played a decisive role in the fall of communism because he confronted the USSR with a dilemma: either a costly arms race or comprehensive democratic reform. Others, however, point to the importance of the dismantling of hostile stereotypes, undertaken by Willy Brandt through the politics of détente and "transformation through rapprochement."

Both are probably right. Two premises of Brandt's politics were nonetheless certainly completely wrong: the conviction that the politics of détente and security was the key to everything, and the view that changes in Eastern Europe could be carried out only by the communist elites. Both of these premises turned out to be false, and they led to political and moral blindness.

Kissinger's détente and Brandt's *Ostpolitik* testified to mediocre understanding of the weaknesses of the Soviet system, and to a lordly nonchalant lack of sensitivity to the aspirations and hopes of Eastern and Central European societies. It is true—détente contributed to the destabilization of communist regimes, but that was not either Kissinger's or Brandt's political goal.

## XI

I try to understand Brandt: a moral politician in the world of real politics. How to combine these two elements—moral values and political pragmatism? It was a dance on a thin rope. He was able to dance on this rope for quite a while. Unblocking relations with the USSR, the GDR, and Poland was wise, honest, and courageous politics. Later Brandt fell into the trap of the politics of "rapprochement through fraternization." He thought that it was the only possible, sensible, and real politics for the future. He consciously ignored the opposition in the USSR, the GDR, and Poland.

In real politics both the ethic of conviction and the ethic of responsibility are important. A balance between the two, however, matters. Brandt lost this balance. It was as if the antifascist and conspirator, dissident and émigré became transformed into a Kissinger-type diplomat.

Brandt was silent on two occasions: while kneeling in front of the Ghetto Heroes Monument in 1970, and while shaking hands with Polish generals in 1985. The first silence was a shocking scream, the second—shameful conformity.

The contradiction between the moral imperative—let us say in the end—and the demand for effectiveness has always existed in the world of politics. The fact that Brandt—in a certain phase of his life—solved this contradiction poorly does not mean that it will cease to exist. The contradiction between witnessing and diplomacy is an irremovable element of politics.

Willy Brandt sought fundamental changes that were revolutionary because they were pursued without resorting to violence. But violence is a temptation and—typically—a logical consequence of revolution. Always a source of hope, revolution often turns into a nightmare for societies. At the end of the twentieth century, Central and Eastern Europe lived through revolutions that were called "velvet." On closer analysis, however, it is easy to conclude that this designation was made too hastily—it is enough to recall Romania, the

Caucasus, the Balkans. The Eastern and Central European anti-communist revolution had two guises: velvet and bloody. This necessitated taking a fresh look at historical revolutions, especially the French Revolution.

Reflection about the dilemmas of historical revolutions was part of ongoing arguments about the present in post-communist countries and, at the same time, about the future of the concepts of freedom, tolerance, and pluralism. Those arguments have not been resolved. This book is a fragment of these broader discussions.

# TWO

# The Trouble with History

I

One of the right-wing weeklies in Poland published a series of articles on McCarthyism, serving as a big apology for the work of Senator Joseph McCarthy and others who instigated the American Red Scare more than fifty years ago. This sad episode in the history of the United States, marked by a triumph of informers and blackmail, a culture of fear, and interrogations—which ended up with the discrediting of Senator McCarthy, an inquisitor searching for communists in the White House, Pentagon, and State Department—has more recently found enthusiasts on the other side of the ocean in Poland, a country that has been priding itself on being a member of the family of democratic states. And it has a right to be proud, because Poland is indeed a democratic country. But this admiration for the work of McCarthy and his followers illustrates well the traps that await the new democracies of the post-communist period. And this does not concern only Poland. Each of those young democracies is susceptible to the illness caused by the peculiar ideological virus that I call the virus of anti-communism with a Bolshevik face. This virus could also be called something else—the virus of fundamentalism, spreading the belief that by using the techniques of intimidating public opinion one can build a world without sin; and that this can only happen if the state is governed by sinless individuals who are equipped with the doctrine of the one and only correct project for organizing human relations.

So what is that one and only correct project? It is a project for fighting the decay that manifests itself as corruption, moral decline, pornography, and pansexuality, abortion and homosexuality, contraception and feminism. This decay also expresses itself as moral relativism, that is, a disbelief in revealed and ultimate truths, which are proclaimed by those in power. It reveals itself as a crisis of national identity that is cosmopolitanism without national belonging, or as contempt for the heroic history of one's own nation. This world in decay is marked by hidden links among the "sinful" people—links that must be destroyed and eliminated right away. This is why controls ought to be tightened, the penal code toughened, and a good nation protected from people immersed in sin. This is also why "the sinless" have to take over the security apparatus, the system of justice, the world of media and financial operations, police records and the education of youth, institutions of culture and the national heritage. And this process of taking over the state by the "party of the sinless" has to be accompanied by a permanent unmasking of the sinful. All of the recent culture and historical knowledge were, after all, created by the sinful, and that is why they are polluted by falsity. For that reason the sinful ought to be exposed and history ought to be written anew. This would be expedited by the recently proclaimed "politics of history."

The politics of history, as its architects proclaim, aims to clear the past of national nihilism and moral relativism. They also proclaim that at the threshold of democratic transformation, it was demanded of Poles (but also Russians, Romanians, Slovaks, et cetera) that they give up their national and historical identity. Today the sinless authors of the politics of history want to bring back this justified pride in the national past. Let us ignore the fact that those statements were false, as nobody ever postulated that kind of nonsensical demand. But what does such a politics of history mean in practice? It means an apologetic relationship to one's own national past. It presents the thesis that all Polish disasters were the result of Polish benevolence, trust, and gentleness, and of the malice and cruelty of foreigners.

Naturally such thinking is not a uniquely Polish phenomenon. This type of historical consciousness exists within any national culture. When it comes to our sins we prefer to be silent or to gloss over them. And whatever is wise and noble we tend to overemphasize—with one exception: the most recent history. To those sinless ones this recent history has been a time of collapse of the moral order, a time of betrayal of the ideals of the national community, a time of contempt for the faith of our ancestors. That is why the "sinless" proclaim the need for a national conservative revolution that will return everything to its rightful place.

This kind of discourse one can hear in every post-communist country from Russia to Albania. In Russia the controversy focuses around the old past, the Tsarist one, and the new past, the Bolshevik—around the appraisals of both Peter and Catherine the Great, Stolypin's reforms, and the February Revolution of 1917. It also concerns the Bolshevik Revolution and appraisals of Lenin and Stalin, and finally of Gorbachev. There appeared in Russia, in the circles of the Kremlin elite, tendencies to formulate the only correct true and canonic and obligatory vision of Russia's history. Would those tendencies transform themselves into a legally decreed official canon of history, it would be a sad end of Russian freedom. Freedom—whether in Russia or anywhere else—means debate, a multiplicity of viewpoints, pluralism of opinion. A monologue is always the privilege of dictatorships.

The monologue was a feature of the communist dictatorship. For us, the people of the democratic opposition, rebellion against communism was a rejection of official lies and of that culture of monologue. In a spirit of dialogue and pluralism, we even rejected the idea of overthrowing the dictatorship. It is clear that communism created as its antithesis not only an attitude of dialogue and pluralism, but also a philosophy of replacing the communist monologue with an anti-communist monologue. According to the spokespersons of this tendency, the post-1989 years of freedom have been polluted by the sin of rotten compromises with the people of the communist regime, with national nihilists of the liberal-left orientation, with Russia and Germany. According to the sinless, it was a sin to have refrained from a radical dealing with the past, for the absence of such de-communization and lustration has prevented an uncompromising appraisal of the past, or the production of an unambiguous statement that communist rule from 1944 to 1989 was simply a Soviet occupation. But was it that, in fact?

II

The truth will liberate you, declared John Paul II, the greatest authority figure for Poles. If this is the case, why do we keep repeating Pontius Pilate's question: "What is the truth about our history?" Is the frequently repeated formula true that after the Nazi occupation came the Soviet occupation?

No, it is not true. One cannot compare the fate of the Polish nation under the Nazi occupation with existence in a satellite state of limited sovereignty like the Polish People's Republic (1945–1989). Similarly, the dismantling of the communist dictatorship had nothing in common with the end of the Nazi occupation. The dismantling of communism in Poland unfolded through the Round Table agreements signed in the spring of 1989. At this table representatives of both the communist regime and the anti-communist opposition sat together, and it was they who made the compromise that opened the road to freedom. In Budapest in October 1956, officers of the communist apparatus were hanged on lampposts. In Poland, not a single window was broken, and the dictatorship was overthrown by the ballot. Poland was the first communist state to gain the capacity to decide about its own fate.

That freedom brought anxiety and insecurity. There were various traditions that coexisted more or less harmoniously within the democratic opposition. There was only one thing everybody agreed on: that the past had to be de-falsified. But while for some that meant an honest accounting of one's own biography, for others de-falsifying the past meant its total rejection. According to that second approach, all of the people in power and those who worked for them ought to be treated as collaborators; all those who after 1945 took part in supporting communist rule were to be labeled Quislings and taken to court for high treason against their own nation. And that was the heart of disagreement. Because if Poland was neither a kind of "General Gouvernement" on the Nazi model nor a "Vistula Land" (Privislanskij Kraj) on the Tsarist model, but a satellite state ruled as a dictatorship, then one had to recognize that Poles who lived in this state satisfied their essential needs and fulfilled their essential interests, though they were not able to do it democratically, as a free people.

To assume such a position, however, means that one has to consider the situation of Polish communists in regard to the Kremlin, their evolution from Stalinist fanaticism and terror to a dictatorship that tolerated an independent Catholic Church and private farming, and periodically allowed some margin of freedom in artistic expression and scholarly research. One must also keep in mind actual human lives, and concrete choices people had to make daily. After all, anybody who wanted to do something beneficial for the community was condemned to some form of collaboration with the communist regime. And it was from among these initially committed communists, the communists of the dictatorship's first decade, that the most insightful, courageous, and consistent critics of communism later emerged.

Can one mechanically classify all of those people as traitors to Poland? Should the writer who supported the communist power in its early years, but later became a symbol of resistance to the dictatorship and a moral authority, be counted as a traitor or included in the pantheon of national heroes? We know that in every communist country there were more than a few such symbolic figures. The reverse also happened: writers who were silent during the Stalinist years, and later supported the communist power, are today eagerly reminding their current adversaries of the latter's earlier involvement. In a word, all sorts of things happened.

The Polish People's Republic had its own complicated prehistory that cannot be reduced to its servitude to the Soviet Union. This prehistory is made up of the Second Republic (1918–1939), which was perceived as an anachronistic quasi-dictatorship, incapable of agricultural and other social reforms, as a country discriminating against national minorities, a country of fraudulent elections and political trials, a country of selfishness and pomposity of the ruling elites. Another issue was the reaction to Nazism, which was perceived as an absolute evil and the result of the total failure of the world's liberal democracies. Finally there was the imposition of communism, which was a result of Poland's betrayal by the Allies at the Yalta Conference. The military hegemony of the Stalinist Soviet Union had, in Polish eyes, the permission of America and Britain. The integral anti-communism of the "sinless" did not want to hear about such nuances or extenuating circumstances—betrayal was betrayal, and as such ought to be severely judged even after sixty years.

The simple result of such a position was de-communization and lustration. De-communization was understood as a ban on holding state jobs by people previously active in the communist apparatus. The question nevertheless arose: was everybody to be included in that ban? Even those who had helped bring about the Round Table and the dismantling of the dictatorship? In such a ban there was a spirit recalling the formula of Jacobins: if you are in power, I demand for myself civil rights, because those are your principles; if I am in power, I take away those rights from you because those are my principles. To break the principle of equality under the law, which after all cannot be retroactive, meant a very peculiar understanding of democratic order. In this way the dispute over the past transformed itself into a fundamental dispute over what ought to be the premise of the founding act of the new state—reconciliation or revenge?

A different aspect of this is apparent in the controversy over lustration—that is, about judging people on the basis of materials held in the Secret Police archives. One could say that those controlling these archives gained the ability to compromise anybody who was an object of police interest, which of course meant, above all, the people of the democratic opposition. I know from my own experience that police agents infiltrated the circles of the opposition, and of course it could not have been otherwise. This is what happens in all situations in which a dictatorship fights the opposition. But is there an acceptable situation in which police reports are more credible testimony about the life of a person from the opposition than the entirety of his or her life? Are those reports more credible than the testimonies of his fellow dissidents? Unfortunately there are historians who think just that.

The crowning touch of this peculiar historiosophy, which connects a conspiratorial vision of the world with "detectivist" materialism, are the publications that accuse Lech Walesa, leader of Solidarity and winner of the Nobel Peace Prize, of being an agent of the secret police. I know it sounds like a gloomy story from a novel by Franz Kafka. But nevertheless we are witnessing how the dispute over communist Poland is transforming itself into a dispute over the assessment of the democratic opposition. Lustration, which was to have been a path to the truth about communism, has become a way of annihilating this truth. Not only with regard to the communists and the secret police, but also with regard to their targeted victims. History as remembered and told by the people of the anti-communist opposition has been replaced with a narrative by informers and police functionaries. One would have thought that the history of the victims could not possibly be written on the basis of evidence provided by the hangmen, but gradually one absurdity overtakes another. The police archives are being searched in a wild and illegal way, exposing various documents that are to prove the collaboration of some Catholic priests with the communist security apparatus, and all of that is done in a crudely uncivil way.

The lustration carnival continues, and a complex past becomes an opportunity to formulate simplistic theories that become tools in a political struggle. It leads to the conclusion that the anti-communist opposition did not really have its own heroes because it was made up of people who only wanted to "fix communism" rather than get rid of it; or else they were simply its agents. The past ceases to be the source of national pride that the sinless called for; the past becomes a baseball bat for destroying political opponents; it becomes a method for intimidating public opinion. The sinless anti-communists with a Bolshevik face believe—as the Jacobins and Bolsheviks did—that it is with them that the new era of national history begins.

III

The dispute over the communist legacy is interwoven with the dispute over the relationships of Poles with their neighbors and national minorities. This is not the place to examine in detail a complicated problem of the Polish-Jewish relationship. No doubt this is the most painful and divisive issue for Polish public opinion. Anti-Semitism will for a long time be a source of conflict in debates about the past. An example was the debate about the massacre in Jedwabne in July 1941. The truth about this crime, committed by a section of the ethnic Polish population upon its Jewish neighbors, shook the entire national mythology of anti-Nazi resistance. This crime, inspired by the Nazis but committed by Polish hands, opened a huge controversy showing two faces of Poland: a noble and courageous face, but also an ugly and mendacious face. Almost the entire historical consciousness of the Poles had to confront this aspect of the truth that people and communities prefer to purge from their memory. The debate over Jedwabne revealed this problem in all its complexity, but of course it did not solve it.

Both the controversy over communism and the controversy over Jedwabne presented Polish Catholicism with a new essential question. And here again we have seen various faces of Catholicism: from the evangelical attitude striving for truth and repentance, to mendacity and hateful denial of the facts. So this is another problem that Polish historical consciousness has to address.

The political role of the Catholic Church is well known, as is its work toward Polish-German reconciliation. In the Polish bishops' famous pastoral letter to their German counterparts (1965), it was written: We extend our hand in a gesture of reconciliation, in a gesture of forgiveness, and we ask for forgiveness as well. This is an extraordinary document that belongs among the most beautiful pages of the Polish historical tradition, and more beautiful for having been difficult, and because of that, rare. We have also witnessed a joint declaration of Polish and Ukrainian bishops——a gesture that gives new meaning to Polish-Ukrainian relations, which were marked by years of mutual hatred and rivers of blood. But also in this case, there was no lack of people on both sides, Polish and Ukrainian, who wanted to use historical memory as an instrument in the struggle for power in their own country. Feeding the spirit of hatred, elevating the memories of wrongs suffered, but at the same time being silent or dishonest about the wrongs we ourselves have committed, are more usual. Historical wounds can only heal in a climate of free debate, in which everyone can cry out about one's own wrongs, pains, and sufferings. The same goes for Polish-Russian relations, interrupted by absurd declarations from the Kremlin regarding, for example, the Ribbentrop-Molotov Pact or the Katyn massacre. The motivation for such statements is clear: it is about relieving internal tensions by creating external ones. Such a policy may serve as an effective manipulation of public opinion, but it certainly does not serve historical truth.

Polish-German relations have been evolving somewhat differently. Reconciliation between Poland and Germany seemed, on one hand, a miracle, and on the other a natural result of the collapse of communism. Though it was clouded by the old controversy over the Berlin Center for the Expellees, there are numerous areas of shared interest that have been worked out harmoniously over the course of the past two decades.

The turn of public opinion toward nationalist-conservative rhetoric has its own clear reflection in controversies among historians. History becomes more and more frequently an instrument creating the conflicts of today. This is why, as it turns out, the role and responsibility of historians acquires new meaning.

IV

The interweaving of history—a teacher of life—and current politics can easily be used to manipulate people's behavior in order to achieve concrete political goals. That has always been the point, after all, of the politics of history. People of my generation remember how certain names disappeared from history textbooks, and certain faces disappeared from historical photographs.

To repeat: the democratic opposition confronted the monologue of the communists' version of history with a polyphonic voice. The official canon was challenged by various historical truths. That is why it seemed beyond question that for the people of the democratic opposition the real teacher of life was history—as it taught that life is a persistent striving toward truth. It taught, namely, that even though no one can call oneself an owner of objective truth about the past, the consciousness of one's own subjectivism and the knowledge of the limitations of one's own view have their own limits. There are many unclear and ambiguous issues, but no reasonable person would say that on September 1, 1939, Poland invaded Germany.

The experience of recent centuries shows that knowledge of history is an irremovable element of national identity and memory—without a sense of their own history, nations degenerate and often disappear. One form of such degeneration is any diktat of falsified history, as it gives birth to an identity built on a lie. For this kind of deformation peoples and nations usually pay a very high price. In order to protect historical consciousness from distortion, anybody who writes about history ought to be loyal to the sources; such a person ought to present to the reader all accessible sources and all prior interpretations of those sources. Historians ought to remember that they are part of the polyphony that accompanies any reflection on the past; they ought to remember that they are not anointed by God to announce revealed truth. Historical sources ought to be equally accessible to all researchers, as only in that way can one in the democratic debate verify the reliability of the argument. Finally, any historical document ought to be subjected to a critical review. As an example of this, the speeches of Hitler concerning the anti-Nazi opposition or those by Stalin on the anti-Stalinist opposition are for the historian a priceless source of knowledge about Hitler and Stalin, but they are not an adequate source of knowledge about the anti-Nazi or the anti-Stalinist opposition. This applies equally to the historian who examines the Gestapo or KGB archives.

History opens up for any national community a path to freedom and to the truth about itself. This freedom is made up of the capacity for autonomous evaluation of the past, the confrontation of various points of view, and various interpretations of the sources. The truth of history is often polyphonic—the same events are differently perceived by differently situated observers. They are variously interpreted by variously thinking researchers. And this polyphony constitutes perhaps the most important truth about the past.

To study and to describe history is always a conversation with the Other, the one who thinks differently, who is differently situated, and who has been differently shaped by his or her social position. To want to understand means to want to understand the other. One cannot understand the French Revolution or the American Civil War by adopting only one perspective, whether monarchist or Jacobin, that of Lincoln or the southern generals. The basic condition for understanding is the juxtaposition of various narratives, and only out of such confrontation can there emerge a picture of the reasons behind any conflict.

The refusal to talk with the Other is at the same time a refusal to understand one's own past, a refusal to face the old evils and betrayals that were committed by my own community. Such refusal is a giving up of one's own freedom and one's own striving for the truth. It is precisely then that history becomes a baseball bat used to whack those who think differently; it becomes a gag forced onto the mouth of the critics. Again: in history there is no one and only truth revealed to the advocates of the ruling party. The kind of patriotism born of the logic of the gag and the baseball bat usually becomes— let's repeat after Samuel Johnson—the last refuge of scoundrels. This type of patriotism also recommends treating historical research and reflection on the past as an expression of concern for "the strengthening of national identity," and for defending Poland's good name in the world. As the advocates of such a "politics of history" understand it, one ought to exhibit the dignified acts in Polish history, and leave out or play down those that are less noble; one could also falsify the description of the ignoble acts to such an extent that they start looking like reasons for pride. In this way one could present discrimination against Jewish youths through the "bench ghetto" and *numerus clausus* of interwar Poland as the national self-defense of Poles endangered by a Jewish invasion. Similarly one could represent discrimination against the Ukrainian population as self-defense against Bolshevism or terrorism. One could present the so-called Brześć trial of the 1930s, which led to the imprisonment of distinguished leaders of the Polish opposition, as an impartial and indispensable act of strengthening our statehood. And all of this out of a concern for the good name of Poland in the world.

But one's good name cannot be defended with the help of lies—the publicly proclaimed lie disgraces the good name of any nation. And the truth—no matter how bitter—liberates critical reflection, personal dignity, and the courage to live in accordance with values.

In recent years history has invaded politics. The dispute over the legacy of fascism, communism, colonialism, and racial discrimination (including apartheid) more and more frequently turns into a dispute concerning moral—as well as material—compensation, which means that it is an argument over money. There is no one prescription that would help to solve the mounting conflicts over the past. History will not cease to be an element of blackmail, a method of humiliating opponents, and a way of disciplining them, for a power apparatus is always polluted by the temptation of authoritarianism.

One is left having to believe that history will continue also to be a realm of encounters between the various memories and sensitivities through which one intends to understand the Other. Any collective consciousness celebrates the memory of great national traditions, but among the ingredients of these traditions are always heretics who conduct an unrelenting debate with that tradition, continuously transforming and enriching it by bringing in their own accomplishments and thus ensuring the eternal vitality of the tradition. It is the guardians of the *only revealed truth* who exterminate tradition, as they turn the subject of the debate into the object of a cult. Their triumphs are a sign of bad news for the democratic debate: the ghost of a patriotic gagging appears. This is why the responsibility of a historian, an intellectual grappling with history, concerned with continuous enrichment of the image of the past, is to cultivate a spirit of heresy, for as Czeslaw Milosz says, "the salt to the times is in the heresy." This is why the historian is required to observe the spirit of both humility and boldness at the same time: humble vis-à-vis values, and bold vis-à-vis the situation. He has to believe that the truth is worth caring for; and that only the truth has the power to liberate.

PART TWO

# THREE

# The Ultras of Moral Revolution

We need a moral revolution!

Do we really need one?

But of course! Replied an ultra-revolutionary, a Jacobin.

But of course! Replied an ultra-reactionary, a partisan of the Counterrevolution.

Radicals, adherents of extreme solutions, Ultras of all the colors of the rainbow, have a need for revolutionary upheavals, because only upheavals that turn the world upside down allow them to fulfill their dream of a great cleansing.

I

The Jacobin, the revolutionary Ultra, says:

We need a moral revolution because we are surrounded by "souls of mud"—reactionaries, hidden royalists, petty individuals, one-day patriots—who are conspiring against our revolutionary government. We need a moral revolution because vice is spreading. Reactionary newspapers are sowing lies; so one has to force them into silence. Corruption is spreading; so we must look carefully at the rich. "I regard wealth," said Robespierre, "not only as the price of crimes, but as a punishment for them; I want to be poor, so as not to be unfortunate." France is surrounded by traitors—those poisonous insects sowing shamelessness, deceit, meanness. It is they who caused the collapse of a state and society functioning according to one system of values, discovered in 1789, with rules that allowed us to maintain a dignity and a brotherhood founded upon the need to do good. We need a moral revolution today, now that we have a chance to leave the crisis of non-memory and the curse of a fresh start. We need a cleansing, which means a capacity to do good for the Revolution. It also means a recognition of one's own errors—one's fatal tolerance for "moderates," for the forgiving and the temperate.

The conservative, the reactionary Ultra, says:

We need a moral revolution because now, after the return of the Bourbons, the tide of revolution has receded. The time has passed when vice ruled triumphant over France; when regicide was a law unto itself; when those responsible for regicide dictated their own laws; when virtue was humiliated, loyalty persecuted, and property confiscated. It's true that a cruel despotism and the omnipotent guillotine, that revolution—this huge gutter of filth—polluted France. Nevertheless France still has many virtues; so one can, wrote Joseph de Maistre, "start the nation anew." France, washed clean from the dirt of Jacobinism, restored to its monarchic and Catholic roots, will become a symbol of reconciliation between the king and his subjects. We need a moral revolution in order to restore the dream of a state and society functioning according to one system of values, with rules that allow us to maintain the loyalty and dignity befitting royal subjects, always inclined to do good. We need a moral revolution because today everything is possible, "even the resurrection of the dead," not to mention the resurrection of "our own moral subjectivity." One must avoid at all costs a compromise with the bastards of Jacobinism and Bonapartism, who want a constitutional monarchy, that is, a king without royal power—they don't understand that "every constitution is regicide."

What familiar voices, despite such different historical costumes. I hear them continuously today—with mounting sadness and amazement. After all, those who echo them ought to know where it all leads.

Does history repeat itself? Karl Marx once wrote, paraphrasing Hegel, that each historical fact repeats itself twice—the original drama turns into farce. Marx was wrong: history repeats itself much more frequently. The world is still full of inquisitors and heretics, liars and those lied to, terrorists and the terrorized. There is still someone dying at Thermopylae, someone drinking a glass of hemlock, someone crossing the Rubicon, someone drawing up a proscription list. And nothing suggests that these things will stop repeating themselves.

We like to reiterate that history is a teacher of life. If this is indeed true, we listen very poorly to its lessons. That is why I am reflecting today on the Ultras of the Revolution and the Ultras of the Counterrevolution, who

dreamed about a big cleansing and a moral revolution
—not so that the language of that reign of terror may
never repeat itself, but because I'm convinced it will inevitably do so.

II

After a victorious civil war, Lucius Cornelius Sulla, the
Roman dictator, began his rule by taking revenge on his
opponents. He did it with a peculiar method, namely,
by ordering the drawing up of proscription lists, that is,
lists of outlawed enemies—and designating a reward
for their heads. In their book *A History of Rome Down to
the Reign of Constantine* (1979), historians Max Cary
and Howard Hayes Scullard wrote that, with a nerve-
racking premeditation, Sulla prolonged the listing of
new victims, announcing from time to time additional
proscription lists. This modernized system of mass
murders was aimed with particular viciousness at those
adversaries who were wealthy. Their property was confiscated, and the cities of Italy became theaters of execution. This was the purpose of the proscription lists
Sulla announced: it was terrifying to find one's name on
such a list.

For centuries the list of names has been an irremovable element of social history: the lists of witches burned at the stake; the lists of heretics examined by the Inquisition; the lists of Jesuits condemned to exile; the lists of Masons; the lists of Jews; the lists of Christians suspected of Jewish background; the lists of communists and those suspected of having communist sympathies; the lists of royalists and other enemies of revolution; the lists of agents of the Tsarist Okhrana; the lists of hostages; and the lists of those beheaded by guillotine or axe, or those who were shot.

Executions were usually preceded by the lists of suspects—those suspected of revolutionary or subversive activities, of a sinful past or present, of betrayal. Suspicion marched ahead of accusation and execution.

### III

The French Revolution overturned an absolute monarchy and established a constitutional monarchy. "This constitution was also vitiated," wrote Hegel, "by the existence of absolute mistrust; the dynasty lay under suspicion, because it had lost the power it formerly enjoyed. . . . Neither government nor constitution could be maintained on this footing, and the ruin of both was the result." And he continues:

A government of some kind, however, is always in existence. The question presents itself then, Whence did it emanate? Theoretically, it proceeded from the people; really and truly, from the National Convention and its Committees. The forces now dominant are the abstract principles—Freedom, and, as it exists within the limits of the Subjective Will—Virtue. This Virtue has now to conduct the government in opposition to the Many, whom their corruption and attachment to old interests, or a liberty that has degenerated into license, and the violence of their passions, render unfaithful to virtue. Virtue here is a simple abstract principle and distinguishes the citizens into two classes only—those who are favorably disposed and those who are not. But disposition can only be recognized and judged of by disposition. *Suspicion* therefore is in the ascendant; but virtue, as soon as it becomes liable to suspicion, is already condemned. Suspicion attained a terrible power and brought to the scaffold the Monarch, whose subjective will was in fact the religious conscience of a Catholic. Robespierre set up the principle of Virtue as supreme, and it may be said that with this man Virtue was an earnest matter. *Virtue* and *Terror* were the order of the day; for Subjective Virtue, whose sway is based on disposition only, brings with it the most fearful tyranny. It exercises its power without legal formalities, and the punishment it inflicts is very simple—*Death*.[1]

And it had begun so beautifully. The Revolution began under a hopeful sign of freedom, equality, and brotherhood. The Bastille—a bastion and symbol of tyranny—was captured. King Louis XVI chose a path of compromise with the revolutionary camp; absolutism collapsed. It looked like "the King with the people, the people with the King."

Speaking parenthetically: in July of 1789, the Bastille, where opponents of the king had been imprisoned, had only seven prisoners—four counterfeiters, two mentally ill, and one imprisoned at the request of his father. Such was this bastion of tyranny. Such a bastion; such a tyranny. It was already absolutism with broken teeth.

In spite of that, a historic event took place, the event of an epoch. The Declaration of the Rights of Man and

Citizen, crafted by the Marquis de Lafayette, proclaimed that people are born and remain free and equal under the law, that they become free as soon as they want to be free. The revolutionaries said it was different in England, where so much blood had been shed, that their revolution had triumphed almost without bloodshed. And they repeated that the Revolution opened the gate through which France advanced from tyranny to freedom.

The Restoration also began beautifully. After a quarter century of revolutionary and Napoleonic turmoil, with the advent of Louis XVIII there started a time of gentle words and conciliatory gestures. François-René de Chateaubriand, the most distinguished Bourbon ideologue, wrote in 1814 that Louis XVIII is "a prince who is known for his enlightened mind, is unsusceptible to prejudice, and is a stranger to vengeance." He quoted the words of Louis XVI: "I forgive with all my heart those who for no reason from my side became my enemies, and I ask God to forgive them." Speaking on behalf of the supporters of the Restoration, Chateaubriand declared: "We want a monarchy based on the principle of equal rights, the principle of morality, civic freedom, political and religious tolerance."

The Restoration did not end in words. Louis XVIII proclaimed a charter that was an act of reconciliation between the Restoration and the Revolution. It guaranteed the inviolability of property from the Napoleonic period and maintained the nobility of the status of the empire; but it also declared the equality of citizens and their fundamental freedoms. And it even promised amnesty to those who were involved in regicide. Louis XVIII wanted to reassure Frenchmen that he did not want revenge, as his enemies claimed. He declared that only a system of moderation could prevent France from tearing itself apart with its own hands.

IV

Every revolution has its own dynamic; each is too slow, unfinished, betrayed. From within each revolution comes a demand for acceleration, completion, protection against betrayal. On the very threshold of the French Revolution the demand that the monarch give in to the National Assembly was revolutionary. A compromise between the Revolution and the monarch on behalf of constitutional rule and a Declaration of the Rights of Man was celebrated as a victory of the revolutionaries. But soon this compromise, built on a dualism—the self-limitation of the monarch in his power and of the Revolution in its demands—turned out to be fragile. The radical monarchists saw in it the capitulation of the king; the radical revolutionaries saw it as a betrayal of their ideals. The Revolution ought to be crushed by the army. The king ought to be removed; long live the Republic, retorted the revolutionary Jacobins.

The Jacobins came out on top. Monarchists escaped abroad, and the king was imprisoned, judged, and guillotined. Any voice against the dissolution of the monarchy—the constitutional one—was called treason, as were voices that demanded a normal judicial process or at least a renunciation of the death penalty. The Revolution, begun in the name of freedom, transformed itself into an aspiration for a republican order against the constitutional monarchy. It was not about freedom anymore but about the Republic, and any critic of this solution was suspected of treason. And the controversy over the Republic transformed itself into a ruthless fight for power in the revolutionary camp.

Every restoration has its own dynamic; each is too slow, unfinished, betrayed. Each restoration hides within itself the guardians of the holy flame of past institutions and customs—the Ultras. The Ultras have to reject any compromise between tradition and revolution, because the Revolution was for them an absolute evil, without a grain of good—the height of absurdity and moral decay. It is "a pure impurity," said Joseph de Maistre. "It is a wonder of decay, a wonder of absurdity, and a wonder of banditry."

For an Ultra then, the Charter of Louis XVIII was nonsense, an absurdity, "a work of madness and darkness." One has to break with the chimera of the Rights of Man, restore censorship and the privileges of the aristocracy. And the Catholic Church has to guard against "the scum of equality." The Ultras clearly had nothing against France tearing itself apart with its own hands.

There is no reason to question the good intentions of the Jacobins, those Ultras of the Revolution. They really wanted to save the Revolution from the royalists, from foreign armies, from superstition, from treason and corruption. They, diligent readers of the Encyclopedists and Jean-Jacques Rousseau, really wanted France to be ruled by virtue.

But in order to fight monarchists and émigré aristocrats, the Jacobins confiscated the aristocrats' properties and closed their newspapers; to win the war, they demanded unity around the revolutionary government and punished anyone who deviated. To remove superstition, they demanded the loyalty of Catholic priests and exiled those who refused to take an oath. To prevent treason and corruption, they announced a "Great Vigilance" with regard to traitors and the corrupt. Moreover, they introduced a law on suspects—each loyal citizen was obliged to denounce suspects. The measure of revolutionary fervor was the number of denunciations. Long lists of suspects were compiled, then long lists of those imprisoned for being suspect. France was taken over by fear. The Reign of Terror had begun. The theater of the revolutionary guillotine was launched.

The Jacobins saw in the guillotine an instrument for the defense of the Revolution. They believed that it was they who were the Revolution and that they were the guarantors of the durability and continuity of the rule of freedom and virtue. This is why they defended their power without scruples, and why any critic was branded a traitor to the Revolution.

It all began with the trial of Louis XVI. Nobody cared to collect any evidence of guilt or observe normal judicial procedures. The king was guilty because he was king. He had to be guillotined; the people had sentenced him through their representatives. A motion was made to ask French citizens whether they supported the carrying out of the death penalty. Antoine-Louis de Saint-Just, a Jacobin Ultra, retorted passionately that the appeal aimed at creating a conflict between the people and the legislature, and therefore a weakening of the people and bringing back the tyrant to his palace. The crime has wings, argued Saint-Just. It will spread. This intrigue to save the king through "votes bought by foreign gold" will win the ear of the people. But the monarchy is an eternal crime, and the monarch is a barbarian, a tyrant, and a foreigner. The public good requires the death of the king, and the only ones who could think otherwise are either allies of the tyrant or people who have been bribed.

After such arguments, which terrorized the National Assembly, the execution of the king was a mere formality. Justice and the public good—as understood by the Jacobins—won out over the logic of mercy, forgiveness, and conciliation.

Not only was Louis XVI guillotined, but symbolically the old order was sentenced to death. The guillotine for the king defined the norms of the new order. Freedom and virtue entered into a marriage with the guillotine.

V

In any revolution the dialectic of moderation and radicalism takes place. At each revolutionary turn, yesterday's radical person turns out to be today's moderate. If he is lucky, he is accused of cowardly opportunism; if he is not lucky, of treason and participation in counterrevolutionary conspiracy.

Vladimir Lenin, quite fluent in revolutions, wrote this about the Girondistes (moderates): "They wanted to deal with autocracy gently, in a reformative way, without hurting the aristocracy, the gentry, the court—without destroying anything." But the Jacobins—according to Lenin—wanted people "to deal with the monarchy and the aristocracy 'in a plebeian way,' mercilessly exterminating the enemies of freedom, strangling by force their resistance, without making any concessions on behalf of the accursed legacy of subjection."

This is how Lenin imagined the Jacobin moral revolution, and this is how—in a Bolshevik way—he implemented it personally. It is not difficult to understand why he glorified Jacobin terror, calling it "plebeian." It is more difficult to understand why the gentle and compromising path of the Girondistes deserved contempt;

and why the Girondistes were still accused of moral relativism, of blurring the boundary between good and evil—why the aspiration to pluralism and compromise with opponents was taken as an abandonment of moral principles.

The Jacobins perceived their adversaries as conspirators against freedom and virtue. In freedom and virtue they believed fanatically, but they understood them in a peculiar way. The symbol of freedom was the capture of the Bastille, from which seven people were freed, while in the prisons of France, ruled by the Jacobins, there were thousands. And virtue? The Reign of Terror, as Friedrich Engels, also interested in the topic of revolution, soberly wrote, was a rule by people who spread fear around them, and on the other hand it was a rule by people who were themselves full of fear. Those cruelties were committed by people who themselves were in fear, and in this way they reassured themselves.

Fear and denunciations, those were the methods of Jacobin virtue.

The Jacobins declared that they defended freedom against treason, against enemy conspiracy, but conspiracy, simply speaking, was opposition to Jacobin rule and the methods of governance applied by the Ultras.

Conspiracy, in the opinion of François Furet, a historian of the Revolution, is an idea typical of the traditional religious mentality, which is accustomed to treating evil as a product of hidden forces. It is also an idea characteristic of revolutionary consciousness. Thanks to this idea, any obstacle could be explained as the result of enemy actions—high prices, food shortages, corruption scandals. The belief in a conspiracy, Furet said, reinforces the horror of the crime because it cannot be admitted, and expresses the cleansing function of its elimination; it frees one from having to point out the perpetrators of the crime and from revealing what their plans were, because one cannot describe perpetrators who are hidden and whose goals are abstract.

Saint-Just unmasked the Girondistes: he said that within the very body of the National Convention conspirators aimed at the restoration of tyranny had built a nest. Their plans were "sinister" and their actions "refined." They were neither courageous nor open enemies of freedom. They spoke its language; they appeared to be its defenders.

The conspirators were unmasked—some of them escaped, the rest were imprisoned. "Not all the imprisoned," explained Saint-Just, "are guilty. The majority of them were just confused. But in the struggle with the conspiracy, the salvation of the nation is the highest law." Then, it is very difficult to distinguish an error from a crime, and one has to sacrifice the freedom of a few in order to save all. A faction of the conspirators, "secretive and politically sophisticated, seemingly caring about freedom and order, skillfully opposed freedom with freedom, did not distinguish inertia from order and peace, nor republican spirit from anarchy." That faction went with the people and freedom to direct them toward its own goals—toward monarchy—"by making current conditions and the horror of these days look repugnant."

This is the language of Saint-Just, whom Albert Camus considered a great man. Robespierre was also called "the Incorruptible," "the Spotless." Yet it is they, Robespierre and Saint-Just, who became symbols of the cruel terror, the monstrosity of informers, and the guillotine, which killed anybody who got in the way.

It is worth remembering that behind the backs of those idealists of cruelty and apostles of terror hovered out-and-out scoundrels, who used revolutionary slogans and the guillotine to settle dirty accounts, to blackmail, and to pursue shady interests. The idealist fanatic is followed by thugs, scoundrels, and hypocrites.

This is the fate of every revolution. But the scoundrel is less interesting—he appears wherever one can fish in murky waters, get rich by informing on others, get promoted through intrigue, get famous by kicking someone who is down.

More interesting is the idealist: this one is ready to give his life for his ideals, but more willingly he puts others to death on behalf of those ideals. Before he puts them to death by guillotine, though, he puts them to death with words. A fanatic idealist, he reaches for mud before he reaches for his sword. Before he exterminates his enemy, he has to dehumanize him, defile him. If the absolutism of Jacobin virtue was to justify absolute terror, then their enemies—the victims of terror—had also to be absolutely evil, the embodiments of total treason and perfect degradation.

Among the Jacobins—including the leaders—were plenty of corrupt people hungry for power, privilege, and money; people guilty of corruption and theft; people with many complexes; ne'er-do-wells; incurable schemers; careerists at the service of any government. For idealists, it could not have been very pleasant. But, as they say in Polish, when you chop wood, the chips fly. If an informer served virtue, his very contribution eliminated all character flaws. If the intriguer hurt the enemies of virtue, the intrigue became the service to the Revolution. The service of virtue manifested itself in only one way: as hatred of the enemies of virtue. Hatred—as Barbara Skarga has recently reminded us—is a feeling that does not know how to look at the world other than from the perspective of negation. Even in what to others seems valuable and important, it notices exclusively trickery and deceit. Because, for one who hates, this is the natural state of the human condition. Hatred does not aim at improving. Quite to the contrary, it favors the existing situation and with satisfaction cites every error and unsuccessful endeavor, confirming the correctness of its attitude. But above all, with such an orientation, it wants to poison everybody around. And it begins to ooze out until it embraces the whole society.

France ruled by the Jacobins was taken over by the madness of searching for enemies and traitors. Informers, revolutionary tribunals, guillotines—everybody was suspect. Denunciations triumphed along with meanness and fear—all in the name of virtue.

In trying to describe the people of hatred, Skarga writes about those who have a dispersed identity, about people who are "weak" and "susceptible to influence," "ambition-driven," "pathetic" people. Indeed, there were plenty of those in Jacobin clubs and revolutionary tribunals. But more fascinating are the strong people, the honest ones, the idealistic, who are blinded by the drug of revolution and transformed into skillful manipulators, cynics of the political game, demagogues of fluent speech and dried-up heart—people of a religious sect transformed into gang of bandits.

The idealist fanatic, the Jacobin Ultra, believed that, by excluding from public life the people of the *ancien régime*, which had been based on the oppression of subjects by the mighty of the world, one could build a better world in accordance with the ideals of Rousseau and through revolutionary methods. Rousseau said, "I hate subjection because it is the source of all evil." The Ultra Jacobin believed that the revolution would help to end all evil. This is why the Jacobin never spoke in his own name; it was in the name of the Revolution and the Nation, in the name of freedom and virtue, in the name of those humiliated by subordination, that he sent to the guillotine people suspected of vice. Virtue is possible and fascinating only when surrounded by vice. This is why the "just and spotless" need popular injustice and all-embracing sin.

The Jacobin "glorifies the poor," observes Hannah Arendt, so that "his praise of suffering as the spring of Virtue" becomes dangerous, usually serving as a "mere pretext for lust for power."[2] Was the Jacobin sincere in declaring his compassion for the poor and the suffering? We have no reason to doubt it. On the other hand, it was not a compassion for any specific, individual persons. The Jacobin identified with the "boundless suffering of the masses," the suffering of millions. "By the same token," wrote Arendt, "Robespierre lost the capacity to establish and hold fast to rapports with persons in their singularity; the ocean of suffering around him" drowned all particular reasons—reasons of friendship, truthfulness, loyalty to principles.[3] The Revolution in the name of virtue and freedom turned into a dictatorship of sacrilegious liars—the Jacobins in power became perfectly indifferent to the fate of individuals who had been victimized or humiliated. Such people could already be sacrificed without scruples in the name of revolutionary cleansing. The cleansing became a purge—a purge that was meant to wash the dirt of hypocrisy and duplicity from the clean face of revolutionary virtue.

"The Revolution," wrote Arendt, "before it proceeded to devour its own children, unmasked them." In the end, "No one is left among the chief actors who does not stand accused, or at least suspected, of corruption, duplicity, betrayal, conspiracy with the court, and accepting money and instructions from London or Vienna."[4]

Preparing the accusation of Danton, Robespierre wrote in his notebook:

> There is in Danton a certain feature which reveals a thankless and petty soul: he praised the recent productions of Desmoulins, at the Jacobins he dared to demand for them freedom of the press, when I suggested to them the privilege of burning. ... When I showed him the system of calumny of the Girondistes, he answered, "What does that matter to me? Public opinion is a whore, posterity is nonsense!" The word Virtue made Danton laugh: "There is no more reliable virtue," he said laughingly, "than that which I cultivate every night with my wife." How could this man, to whom any moral idea was alien, be a defender of Freedom? Another maxim of Danton's was that one ought to use rascals; that is why he was surrounded by the dirtiest intrigants. He believed in a tolerance for vice, which was to ensure him as many supporters as there are corrupted

people in this world. . . . At every time of crisis Danton took a vacation, when the Jacobins were cursed, he remained silent. When he was attacked himself, he forgave. All the time he appeared to the Girondistes as a tolerant mediator, he bragged publicly that he had never denounced any enemy of freedom, he constantly reached out to them with an olive branch. . . . He did not want the death of the tyrant; he wanted people to be satisfied with his exile. . . . He desired amnesty for all of the guilty; therefore he wanted counter-revolution.[5]

This is an accounting of Danton's crimes drafted by Robespierre. A close friend of Danton said to the Jacobins: if you kill the Girondistes, the next ones will do the same with you. And that is what happened. The day before his execution Danton was to say: "In revolutions power remains at the end with the biggest scoundrels." Led to the square where the guillotine loomed, he was to shout, "Robespierre! You will be following me!" And that is what happened four months later. Louis-Auguste Blanqui, an icon of French revolutionaries in the nineteenth century, imprisoned in 1848, prepared a ruthlessly honest portrait of Robespierre, whom he called "a would-be Napoleon." He wrote that no other personality was as destructive as he was; when he demanded that others give up their personal dreams, it was only so that they could put them onto the altar of his own pride. The National Convention, the highest revolutionary power, he said, was like a herd speechless from fear, standing at the gate to the slaughterhouse. All tongues were frozen, all eyes were glazed, all gestures were petrified in horror.

Robespierre declared: "We need to instill in each person a religious respect for man, this deep sense of obligation that constitutes the only guarantee for introducing a state of social happiness." Blanqui commented:

> It was apparently in order to instill religious respect
> of man for man that Robespierre sent to the guillo-
> tine all his rivals, including the least dangerous op-
> ponents. A furtive glance was enough to send his
> best friend to the guillotine. Camille Desmoulins, a
> friend from youth and a comrade in the struggle and
> an admirer, was executed because he dared to say
> "Burning is not the way to answer."[6]

All of those godlike warriors were cruel people, hungry for power, armed with hypocrisy and their blessed stilettos. Robespierre, mercilessly beheading all those who opposed his ambitions or awakened distrust, constantly presented himself as a victim. On the heaps of corpses murdered by his hand, he consistently repeated the pathetic refrain of Socrates: "They want to force me to drink hemlock . . . and I know that I will drink it." A magnificent pretext for serving it to his opponents.

For Robespierre, the end justified the means, even the most vicious means, when the real goal, wrote Blanqui, was "the desire for power."

## VI

But every restoration also swings from moderation to radicalism. Every restoration is unfinished, inconsistent; it does not fulfill the expectations of its supporters.

After initial declarations on behalf of moderation, conciliation, and accord comes a moment when the Ultras of restoration—also known as White Jacobins—feel disappointed. In France, after a short honeymoon, Napoleon returned to power for a hundred days; after those hundred days, the Ultras retaliated against the thankless French. If the symbol of the beginning of restoration were the appeals to forget about the hatred dividing France, now the Ultras declared that conciliatory

Louis XVIII was a "Jacobin with a lily." They called to stop the appeals for reconciliation because there can be no reconciliation between the party of the hangmen and the party of the victims. The time of doing justice had begun—in the name, of course, of the great cleansing of France from this hellish dirt of both the Revolution and the empire. Because—the Ultra argued—revolution was the child of haughtiness and madness, which fed upon corpses; it was a monster enjoying looting, arson, and butchering. Now one ought to bring back the old prerevolutionary laws, customs, and privileges for the gentry, aristocracy, and the Church—as well as discipline and censorship. "The freedom to print and freedom of the press," said the Ultra, "are the most horrible plagues of our unfortunate times."

And he was sincere in these confessions: he believed that the return to the prerevolutionary golden age is necessary and realistic, but he warned that the revolutionary forces are still powerful, that the majority of the positions in the administration are still occupied by Jacobins and Bonapartists. This is why a great cleansing is needed. "The time for handling with kid gloves is over!"

And indeed it was over. The White Terror flooded France with blood; paramilitary units of royalist guerrillas introduced a climate of vengeance, inquisition, and repression aimed at all suspects; and anybody could be suspected of Jacobinism, of Bonapartism, of anything. In Avignon, the Napoleonic Marshal Brune was murdered. His body was dragged down the street and thrown into the Rhone. The royal government released proscription lists of enemies; censorship was restored. A ban was announced on "provocative shouting and subversive journals." The newly created lists of suspects were kept secret. After the first trials, the first heads rolled. The acts of the executioner brought order and calm. "There is a need for chains, hangmen, torturers, death; let the heads of the Jacobins roll; there is the need for a fear that redeems."

Among those the Chamber of Peers judged was a famous Napoleonic Marshal, Michel Ney. The perfidy of this trial was that those who were to sentence him were his comrades-in-arms. And it was to be chaired by Marshal Jeannot de Moncey. Distressed by the situation, de Moncey sent a letter to Louis XVIII in which he wrote: "Allow me to ask His Majesty, where were his accusers when Ney was fighting on so many battlefields? Can France forget about a hero of the Bersina battle? Am I to put to death someone who has saved so many French lives? I know that I am arousing the hatred of the courtiers, but standing near my grave, I can say, like one of your distinguished ancestors: 'All lost but honor.' I will die satisfied." For these words de Moncey was thrown out of the Chamber of Peers and locked up in a fortress.

The witness for the defense was Marshal Louis-Nicolas Davout, who defended Ney to the very end. Unfortunately, other marshals were short on honor and courage. So Ney was sentenced and shot. In the name of the restoration of knightly virtues, people were used who had behaved despicably, choosing obsequiousness, cowardice, and betrayal.

The violence that was to guarantee virtue became an instrument of villainy. The moderate and the lenient in the camp of restoration were losing; the Ultras were winning. Their restoration was to be the Grand Counterrevolution, that is, revolution—also moral—with a minus sign. All changes introduced by the Revolution were to be erased; all the chimeras of the philosophers of the Enlightenment concerning the state of nature, the social contract, the constitution, the rights of man and the citizen, and parliamentary representation were to be abandoned. The absolute monarchy was to be restored, as this was the only way to return to God's order guarded by the Catholic Church.

Tradition provided an easy model: the Inquisition. The Spanish Inquisition, argued the Ultra, understood that one needs to beat to death any serious attempt against religion. Nobody has the right to criticize the kings of Spain. They know their enemies, and under the law they can punish them. Nobody ought to feel sorry for evildoers, who deserve the punishment for questioning Spanish dogmas. Those who spread heresies ought to be put among the worst criminals. After all, heresy led Europe to the Thirty Years' War. If there had been an active Inquisition in France, the Revolution would never have happened. Therefore, the ruler who refrains from using the stakes of the Inquisition deals a deadly blow to humanity. "The Inquisition on its own," argued de Maistre, the perfect Ultra, "is a blessed institution that provides Spain with an extraordinary service which a sectarian and philosophical fanaticism has derided and shamelessly defamed."

The direct consequence of such reasoning was a law on sacrilege that the Ultras introduced during the Restoration. It stated that "sacrilege is recognized as any active insult to religion made consciously and out of hatred. The profanation of Church vessels is subject to the death penalty. The profanation of consecrated bread calls for the same punishment as parricide." We should add that those guilty of parricide first have their hand cut off and then their head. The Ultra argued eagerly that "as far as someone guilty of sacrilege is concerned, in sentencing him to death one is after all simply sending him to face his natural judge." The author of those words, Louis-Gabriel Bonald, a philosopher of the Ultra camp, certainly believed that it would serve the cleansing and the moral revolution.

Chateaubriand—an unquestioned legitimist—tried unsuccessfully to argue that the principle of religion is mercy, and if it needs the guillotine it is only a triumph for the Church's martyrs. The Ultras won. They believed that only the use of similarly forceful means could prevent huge political defeats and push back particularly forceful attacks on the state. And the most effective of those means was violence; it is violence that creates order, "that stops the hand of man, and threatens with chains, with the sword, with the knout, and with the guillotine." Against rebels one ought to send "soldiers and executioners."

The executioner is the guarantor of order; he struggles with chaos, dirt, and rebellion. The executioner is a man who metes out punishment.

De Maistre asked:

Who is this inexplicable being, who, when there are so many agreeable, lucrative, honest and even honourable professions to choose among, in which a man can exercise his skill or his powers, has chosen that of torturing or killing his own kind? . . .

Hardly has he been assigned to his proper dwelling-place, hardly has he taken possession of it, when others remove their homes elsewhere whence they can no longer see him. . . . The gloomy signal is given; an abject servitor of justice knocks on his door to tell him that he is wanted; he goes; he arrives in a public square covered by a dense, trembling mob. A poisoner, a parricide, a man who has committed sacrilege is tossed to him: he seizes him, stretches him, ties him to a horizontal cross, he raises his arm; there is a horrible silence; there is no sound but that of bones cracking under the bars, and the shrieks of the victim. He unties him. He puts him on the wheel; the shattered limbs are entangled in the spokes; the head hangs down; the hair stands up, and the mouth gaping open like a furnace from time to time emits only a few

bloodstained words to beg for death. He has
finished. . . .

And yet all greatness, all power, all subordination rest on the executioner. He is the terror and the
bond of human association. Remove this mysterious
agent from the world, and in an instant order yields
to chaos: thrones fall, society disappears. God, who
has created sovereignty, has also made punishment;
he has fixed the earth upon these two poles: "For
Jehovah is master of the twin poles and upon them
he maketh turn the world" . . .[7]

"Translating this apology of the executioner," the
modernist writer Bolesław Miciński wrote in an essay,
"On Hatred, Cruelty, and Abstraction," "I had the
impression that my fingers were stained with blood."[8]

"One must analyze the style of this excerpt to
notice," wrote Miciński, "that the source of this spirit is
sadism." From behind the mask of the defender of conservative principles, "the face of a sadist appears." And
also the conviction arises that "man is evil and must
therefore be ruled with an iron truncheon."[9]

So much for Miciński. Isaiah Berlin, after reading
*The Saint Petersburg Dialogues*, observed that de Maistre

is sincerely convinced that "men can only be saved by being hemmed in by the terror of the authorities [and] must be purged by perpetual suffering, must be humbled by being made conscious of their stupidity, malice, and helplessness at every turn.... Their appointed masters must do the duty laid upon them by their maker who has made nature a hierarchical order by the ruthless imposition of the rules—not sparing themselves—and equally ruthless extermination of the enemy."[10] All in the name of moral counterrevolution and cleansing.

## VII

Who is the enemy poisoning the order of freedom and virtue during the Revolution? Who is the enemy destroying God's order on earth and the established hierarchy with Christ's envoy at the top? The Red Ultra will answer the same way as the White Jacobin: This enemy is a sect. There exists in France a political sect, argued Saint-Just. This sect that poisons public life is made out of monarchists both open and hidden, who wanted to remove Louis XVI but did not want to end the monarchy. Today the members of this sect demand moderation and leniency, amnesty for the enemies, and reconciliation with the enemies of virtue. Those people are criminal and arrogant; they are émigrés and British agents. They are corrupted and depraved, thieves, bribe-takers, and dishonest speculators; people who are weak and vain, malcontents and sowers of disagreement, hypocrites and fruitless shouters.

Public life is entangled in the web of this sect. Should not such a society—in which self-interest and envy are the hidden springs of many enemies and criminals who through bribery want to escape justice—launch the greatest possible effort to cleanse itself? And those who try to stop this cleansing, are they not trying to corrupt society? And those who want to corrupt it, are they not trying to destroy it?

There is no hope of prosperity, explained Saint-Just, if the last enemy of freedom would breathe; you ought to punish not only traitors but also those who are neutral; you ought to punish everyone in the Republic who is passive and does not do anything for it. The flame of freedom would cleanse us just as liquid crude iron throws off any dirt. This is why he appealed for everybody to return to moral principles, and for terror to be used against the enemies. It was time to wipe out the enemies of the people "who favor crime and the passions of the depraved." In this way Saint-Just declared war on the sect and announced a great cleansing and moral revolution.

And what was "the sect" for de Maistre? They are those who try to corrupt people or overthrow the existing order. "They are the disturbers and subverts," wrote Berlin. "To the Protestants and Jansenists he now adds Deists and Atheists, Freemasons and Jews, Scientists and Democrats, Jacobins, Liberals, Utilitarians, Anti-clericals, Egalitarians, Perfectibilians, Materialists, Idealists, Lawyers, Journalists, Secular Reformers, and intellectuals of every breed; all those who appeal to abstract principles, who put faith in individual reason or individual conscience; believers in individual liberty or the rational organization of society, reformers and revolutionaries: these are the enemy of the settled order and must be rooted out at all costs. This is '*la secte*,' and it never sleeps; it is forever boring from within."[11]

This sect ought to be annihilated by force, firmly and mercilessly, in the name of the divine order. De Maistre—like any conservative—was convinced that those who launch revolutions in the name of freedom end up as tyrants. Summarizing the Jacobins' doctrine, he remarked sarcastically what people hear from their leaders: "You think that you do not want this law, but we want to assure you that in fact you really desire it. If you dare to reject it, we will punish you by shooting you for not wanting what you want." And that is what they do, concluded de Maistre.

One ought to agree with this "White Jacobin," the most distinguished of the Ultras. This is exactly how the Jacobins, the Red Ultras, acted. They proclaimed themselves the emancipation of freedom and virtue; they privatized the Revolution in order to privatize the nation. The guillotine caused all the French people to become the property of the Revolution. But the White Ultras privatized God and proclaimed themselves the emancipation of the evangelical teachings, while undertaking, intellectually and practically, an effort to convert the French using the executioner's axe.

Blanqui accused Robespierre of sending to the guillotine spokesmen of atheism in order to win back the favor of the Church. This is why he presented as an offering to Catholic priests the head of Chaumette, a preacher of atheism. Blanqui wrote: "What a pleasant surprise it was for the sons and heirs of the Inquisition to see that God had again found Himself under the care of the guillotine. The beautiful times of the mightiness of the divine spirit could be reborn as heads rolled to honor the immortality of the soul. Heretics were made dependent upon the supreme ruler of the torturer. The guillotine had replaced the stake."

Let us set aside the tone of anticlericalism typical of French revolutionary circles, here carried *ad absurdum*, because it is absurd to think that Catholic priests appreciated the cult of the Supreme Being created by Robespierre. Let us emphasize, rather, the well-captured intimate relationship between the guillotine and the stake. The guillotine of the Jacobins was the natural daughter of the Inquisition's stake. And it doesn't really matter at this point that it was an illegitimate daughter. Both the stake and the guillotine were to serve the cleansing, moral revolution, but they have always served the arbitrary claims of the authorities, convinced that they have absolute virtue at their disposal.

And such thinking has always ended badly.

## VIII

The Red Ultras, whether Robespierre or Saint-Just, have legions of defenders. So does the White Jacobin de Maistre. The defenders emphasize that Robespierre was spotless, incorruptible, indomitable; that Saint-Just, a fascinating dreamer, was a good and pure man;

that de Maistre was famous for his personal charm and kindness toward people, and that his apology for the executioner was the result of his horror at the Jacobin terror, a kind of revenge, as he saw in the victim of the executioner either Robespierre or Saint-Just, not just an ordinary mortal.

I gladly agree with the advocates of the Red Ultras and the White Jacobins. But in the rhetoric and mentality of the Red Ultras we can recognize, after all, the early outlines of the rhetoric and mentality of the Bolsheviks; in the icon of Robespierre we can see Lenin and Stalin; and in the terror of the Jacobin guillotine we can see a preview of the platoons of Cheka death squads.[12]

On the other hand, in the catalog of opponents of the divine order prepared by de Maistre we see the same people twentieth-century Fascism added to its enemy list. "De Maistre's violent hatred of free traffic in ideas," wrote Isaiah Berlin, "and his contempt for all intellectuals, are not mere conservatism, . . . but something at once much older and much newer—something that at once echoes the fanatical voices of the Inquisition, and sounds what is perhaps the earliest note of the militant anti-rational Fascism of modern times."[13]

You will say that those are just words, just ideas, written down on paper. But words are not innocent. They have a life of their own. Words create a system of ethical and intellectual interpretation of the world, an interpretation that allows one to see in the guillotine a gate to freedom and virtue and in the executioner's axe a path to God. The history of the Jacobins and Ultras, Red or White, teaches us that there is a need for ethical knowledge, that there are no honest values that would justify reaching for such peculiarly dishonest means and methods. This is why one cannot put people down in the name of lifting them up; this is why one cannot spread the poison of fear in the name of virtue and moral revolution; this is why one cannot push the drug of suspicion in the name of truth and cleansing. This is why one cannot forget that God did not give any person power over any other person; that no one should give up caring about one's own salvation in caring about someone else's salvation; that one cannot force anyone into faith either through force or blackmail; and that the cross is the symbol of the Lord's suffering, not a baseball bat for clubbing adversaries.

I already hear the ironic commentaries: those are the nauseating platitudes of an aesthete, empty moralizing that does not wish to understand that revolution has its rights.

Jacobins and Ultras always reply the same way. After all, to be a Jacobin is to transcend limits. It means to attack the constitution in the name of utopia, and the republic in the name of a perfect republic. It means to criticize the guillotine for being too gentle to enemies; to label the partisans of moderation traitors of the revolution; to be redder than the Reds, more plebeian than the plebeians, more "mad" than the extreme radicals, more vigilant than the tribunals of vigilantism, more suspicious than the lieutenants of suspicion. To be opponents of the death penalty while ordering new executions daily; to be such a relentless hound of the "tolerant" left that one finds oneself to the left of common sense; to be such an enthusiastic defender of the Revolution that one sends other revolutionaries to the guillotine.

"To be ultra," wrote Victor Hugo,

is to go beyond. It is to attack the scepter in the name of the throne, and the mitre in the name of the attar; it is to ill-treat the thing which one is dragging, it is to kick over the traces; it is to cavil at the fagot on the score of the amount of cooking received by heretics; it is to reproach the idol with its small amount of idolatry; it is to insult through excess of respect; it is to discover that the Pope is not sufficiently papish, that the King is not sufficiently royal, and that the night has too much light; it is to be discontented with alabaster, with snow, with the swan and the lily in the name of whiteness; it is to be a partisan of things to the point of becoming their enemy; it is to be so strongly for, as to be against.[14]

The Jacobin and the Ultra will agree on one thing: when one chops the wood, chips fly. Well, I am such a chip. And before I am treated like such a chip by moral revolutionaries in the name of virtue and freedom, in the name of the divine order and revealed truth, allow me to say, "Proceed without me, ladies and gentlemen. I have already learned this lesson." Then you will ask me, "Do you know, you malcontent from the sect of the eternally dissatisfied and afraid, any revolution that would be different?" And I would answer, "Well, there have been different revolutions . . ."

The English Revolution of 1689 was called the Glorious Revolution, and not because of heroic acts and victorious battles, or even because of a victory over a stupid monarch. "The true glory of the British revolution," wrote George Macaulay Trevelyan, "lay in the fact that it was bloodless, that there was no civil war, no massacre, no proscription, and above all that a settlement by consent was reached of the religious and political differences."[15] This settlement stood the test of time; it stabilized freedom in political life and practical compromise in the world of religious passions.

"The men of 1689 were not heroes. Few of them were even honest men. But they were very clever men, and, taught by bitter experience, they behaved at this supreme crisis as very clever men do not always behave, with sense and moderation."[16]

This dangerous situation compelled the bickering Whigs and Tories to make a compromise known as the Revolution Settlement. This was accompanied by the Toleration Act, in which some saw the right to live according to one's conscience, and others "a necessary compromise with error."[17] That compromise ended "continuous and mass sufferings, hatreds and wrongs."

"After a thousand years," concluded Trevelyan, "religion was at length released from the obligation to practice cruelty on principle, by the admission that it is the incorrigible nature of man to hold different opinions on speculative subjects."[18]

The Toleration Act will be called by this historian "a curious patchwork of compromise, illogicality, and political good sense."[19] Wise Britons, wise Macaulay Trevelyan.

IX

We, the malcontents from the sects of the eternally unsatisfied and afraid, dream of something similar. We do not want further moral revolutions; a tightening of the reins; special commissions to track down the enemies of virtue or the divine order; the proscription list of enemies, those who are suspected of animosity. We the malcontents dream of just such a patchwork of compromise and good sense. We the malcontents do not want further revolutions in a country that has not yet recovered from the last several of them.

# FOUR

# Will You Be a True Scoundrel?

## I

In the unfinished novel *Lucien Leuwen* by Stendhal, the well-known Parisian banker Leuwen Senior asks his son, Lucien: "Will you be a true scoundrel to hold this office? . . . —a great career awaits you, as the fools say; but the point is, are you enough of a true scoundrel to manage it? . . . There is this principle: every government always lies. . . . Joining the civil service at the ministry, you have to leave morality at the door."[1] Here you have a bit of non-sentimental education. Such was the creed and the canon of moral and political theology of the French elite of the Restoration period.

The question posed by the father Leuwen belongs to that class of questions that transcend Stendhal's time: How do you want to live? That question is asked by all the main characters in his novels—Julien Sorel, Fabrice del Dongo, Lucien Leuwen. It was asked by Stendhal himself; we ask the same questions of ourselves.

Leuwen Senior is cynical and depraved, but we cannot accuse him of insincerity. It is owing to sincerity that the dialogue between a corrupt banker and his idealistic son, full of belief in freedom and the republican fraternity, sounds so contemporary. The question asked by the elder Leuwen springs out immediately whenever the world, and people's behaviors, habits, and dreams alongside it, is subject to tremendous changes. They are preceded by great anticipation but also by great fear. The changes bring with them great expectations and great suffering; and they are followed by the inevitable great disappointment. Then we say that the people have been deceived and that the ideal has been smashed on the cobblestones.

So it was back then and it has happened often afterwards. And when we realize with bitterness that the

time of scoundrels has arrived and the ideal has plum-
meted all the way down, we start nostalgically remembering the past: for some, the period of glory and fame;
for others, the time of hopes and dreams.

In those long-awaited August days of 1980 the sun
rose above my country. For decades, the oppression had
humiliated us, the hypocritical education stupefied us,
the fear humbled us, and the helpless rebellion frus-
trated us. The atrocities of the Stalinist years enslaved
our senses and our minds and forced us to constant
caution and mistrust, and made us meek and obedient.
We were the people wearing masks, the people of hide-
outs. We lived saddened with the moral ugliness of everyday, trapped in our hopelessness, and completely
alone in the crowd of noisy May Day parades. Only a
few of us uttered the words of dissent and rebellion,
refused to perform the ritual bow, and with determina-
tion signed consecutive protests addressed to the authorities. So few were those rebels that they must have
seemed deplorable and ridiculous. Their hopeless words
and gestures were disregarded, and it was said that
they could have been made invisible by covering them
with a few police hoods. They were perceived—we
were perceived—as an anachronism not even worth a

moment of attention or consideration. All true, until those August days . . .

In August 1980, one year after the first visit of John Paul II, we discarded our masks, we came out of hiding, and we emphatically said "No!" to find that it was the voice of a free and sovereign Poland. What followed were several months of a wonderful Polish carnival ended by mass arrests on the night of December 13, 1981—the first act of martial law. This lasted a long time: seven long years of vegetation under the whip of generals and party secretaries. Finally the year 1989 came—first the Round Table Talks and then the June elections. Firmly, calmly, and with dignity we rejected the order of the communist dictatorship. Freedom had arrived. Every one of us had imagined it differently and expected something different from it. But everyone perceived it as some sort of a moral rebirth. It was to be a movement for something and not against anything.

Today we ask: What had happened to us? Why have we changed the human rights charter into a credit card and why do we reach less willingly for Joseph Conrad's *Lord Jim* or Albert Camus' *The Plague*, the books of our dreams in those years, than for our own checkbooks, the books of our dreams in these times? Why hasn't the evangelical and papal appeal "Fight evil with good!" convinced the deplorable organizers of consecutive witch-hunts and devotees to the truth contained in the secret service archives?

We do not like this world of ours today. We feel bad in this world of ours. Why is that? That world seems so trivial, hard, and cowardly. Nearly everyone goes through huge disappointment, just like in years past, in Stendhal's era, during the period of the Restoration that followed the great French Revolution and the mighty Napoleon. I felt the desire to enter that world, now long-gone, and meet those people, to see their sadness and their angry faces, and to listen to their complaints about living in their own times. I grew to like those walks with Stendhal and Chateaubriand, with Julien Sorel and Lucien Leuwen, and I became interested in their observations and anxieties. How did they perceive that transformation from grandeur into littleness, or that of bravery into intrigue and servility? What was their reaction when the ethos of solidarity of the Bastille conquerors kept transforming into the cult of money, while the ethos of the chivalrous Napoleonic soldiers was exchanged for the divinity of stock exchange quotations?

II

The epoch of Restoration, as perceived by Stendhal, was an epoch without thought. It was also an epoch of boredom. But it was not the common boredom that accompanies everyday conversation between mindless people. This boredom was a specific phenomenon produced by Restoration; it was boredom born of pointlessness and ignobility.

Stendhal often talked about boredom and ignobility in a highly realistic and sarcastic way. Public ritual gestures and clichés were accompanied by secret intrigues, bribes, and denunciations. Stendhal could not stand any of it. He was a man of revolution in the same vein as Napoleon, and he witnessed events that intrigued people and changed the world. His protagonist, Julien Sorel, also loved Napoleon. He would say that it was worthy to live and suffer for Napoleon. How sweet it was to climb the ladder of fortune amongst all that danger. For young people Napoleon was providence itself— even a bricklayer could become an officer or a general. Never before was France so respected by the peoples as during his reign. The recent memory of somebody so great only multiplies the feeling of today's nothingness.

What can Julien possibly expect today, in a futile and thoughtless era? What else, apart from that filthy career?

### III

"Never since the sun had stood in the firmament and the planets revolved around him," wrote Hegel on the French Revolution, "had it been perceived that man's existence centers in his head, i.e. in thought, inspired by which he builds up the world of reality . . . not until now had man advanced to the recognition of the principle that thought ought to govern spiritual reality. This was accordingly a glorious mental dawn. All thinking being shared in the jubilation of this epoch. Emotions of a lofty character stirred men's minds at that time; a spiritual enthusiasm thrilled through the world, as if the reconciliation between the divine and the secular was now first accomplished."[2]

The Hegelian analysis effectively describes the pathos of the epoch. It was then that the foundations of the world were about to change. It was the time of rebellion and arms raised in the air, the tyrant feared the strike, and the wretched of the earth stood up amongst the shining rays of new thought. The revolutionary "La

Marseillaise" and the Napoleonic eagles shaped Stendhal's way of thinking. It is no wonder then that he could not bear listening to the monologues about "Louis XVI condemned to death by the bad people."

The Restoration after Napoleonic rule was for people of the revolution and Napoleon's soldiers simply a time of littleness, pettiness, and venality. "To plunge from Bonaparte and the Empire into what followed them, is to plunge from reality into nothingness, from the summit of a mountain into the gulf."[3] This opinion was voiced by Chateaubriand, a monarchist, a critic of Napoleon, a Bourbon adherent, and certainly not a Jacobin or a liberal. One simply cannot be surprised by Stendhal's stinging reflections. It was Napoleon, after all, now demeaned and kicked around, who made every man feel like the architect of his own fortune and that something could actually be gained through bravery, talent, and wisdom, and not only through birthright and money.

Stendhal loved Napoleon dearly but with no illusions. He remembered well the sycophants swarming around the beloved emperor. It was just like it always had been: the good emperor surrounded by mean courtiers. The emperor registered fantastic victories and, at the same time, the intrigues of the ruling entourage made the imperial court push the motherland into the shade. France was tired with the arrogance of the courtiers, prefects, and mayors. Many of them proved their valor in battle but were mostly obedient toward their superiors and could never be accused of thinking independently. A shade of hypocrisy dominated their dispositions, which was "a clear trace of the empire and its servility." And their road to gaining the general's epaulettes was highly complicated—from the army of revolutionary *sans-culottes* to the faithful service for the emperor. They once swore on their hatred toward all monarchs and now they had to kowtow to imperial marshals. And so, step by step, year by year, the Napoleonic hero gave way to a profiteer. He joined the hussars in 1794. He was just eighteen years old then. He participated in all the war campaigns of the revolution. For the first six years, he thought gallantly and passionately sang "La Marseillaise." However, when Bonaparte named himself consul, the Napoleonic hero, not exactly devoid of innate and acquired cleverness, sensed that "La Marseillaise" was going out of fashion and perhaps should not be sung too often. He read the signs of time correctly—he was the first lieutenant in his regiment who was awarded a medal. But once the emperor was dethroned and the Bourbons returned, he received his first communion and was bestowed the Legion of Honor.

This is not to say that servility was somehow confined to the category of the military and the courtiers. Men of letters were second to none in that respect. Former democrats became champions of kowtowing. The astronomer Pierre Simon de Laplace was an example of "utter wickedness." The famous zoologist Georges Cuvier was "simply disgusted with his servility towards the authority." Many a famous scholar belonged to the category that "made a name for themselves through wickedness." Why this pettiness amongst the great academics? They stood assured of the glory of their writings and were convinced that the scholar would certainly disguise the political opportunist, while in matters of money and medals they were purely utilitarian. But how many despicable bows they had to take in order to secure those medals! "What villainy, what wickedness!" noted Stendhal some years later. "What an abyss of villainy and cowardice." I would repeat after Julien: "Canaille! Canaille! Canaille!"[4]

IV

So who was Napoleon, this Corsican who changed the world?

A conservative would say, and I am summarizing Paul Johnson's argument from *The Birth of the Modern*, that Napoleon was a great lawgiver, a great reformer, a builder of roads, and, occasionally, a state patron, but his conduct was a harbinger of the frightening totalitarian regimes to come in the twentieth century. He definitely cannot be called a democrat. In his eyes, the people were just the ignorant rabble, the *canaille*, who can be dispersed by a salvo of the case-shots. The constitutions designed by Napoleon gave the people fewer electoral rights than the election laws of the *ancien régime*, which in 1789 had called to life the States-General, and they were based on the antidemocratic principle that trust comes from below, power from above. Napoleon did not support individual freedom. In reality, he created the first modern police state.

Hegel, when watching Napoleon in Jena, wrote: "I saw Napoleon, the soul of the world, riding through the town on a reconnaissance."[5] Later, he changed his opinion and called Napoleon "the scourge of God." Adam

Mickiewicz, an émigré in Paris, once said: "Napoleon broke and destroyed old governments, he felt that the matter of freedom is a European issue and that all of Europe should be involved." And the French loved their emperor. It was Napoleon who made the world, including Stendhal himself, witness the greatness of France. That Corsican usurper revolutionized the world. It is true that this soldier and lawgiver changed the republic into an empire, freedom into autocracy, and rights of man into a dictatorship of a despot, but he had the greatness of a victor and conqueror, the explorer of new horizons, and a man who modernized the planet. Stendhal, concluding *Memoirs of an Egotist*, wrote of himself that he respected only man—Napoleon.

The Bourbons had worked hard to earn this kind of love for Napoleon from Stendhal and the French. Once they returned to power after the defeat of the empire, they proved on a nearly daily basis that they had not comprehended or learned anything whatsoever. Such is life—no one can ever do so much to bring back the good name to a fallen ruler than his miserable successors. Disgusted with Bourbon rule, burgher democrats, as described by Andrzej Zahorski in his great essay on France in the years 1815–1848, completely forgot Napoleon's imperial diktat and discovered in him the precursor of democratic liberties.

The Restoration meant a return of expelled Bourbons, the revenge of royalists against the revolution and the empire, the elevation of aristocrats, clericalists, and immigrants, and a degradation of freedom, equality, and fraternity, as well as the glory of the Napoleonic eagles. It was believed that Paris has been defiled by the Bourbons. Stendhal and people like him were willing to forgive Napoleon his diktat and censorship on behalf of his greatness, which in turn made France great. The Bourbon diktat and censorship defended only the pettiness of the Restoration.

Let's see: this sensible and righteous man buys a printing house in the capital of a department and starts a daily. The congregation—similar to the contemporary Catholic Action—decides to ruin him. His license is taken away and the daily is shut down. Faced with this predicament, the man writes a letter to the local mayor and his former friend. The mayor gives him a reply "worthy of a Roman": "Should Mr. Minister allow me the privilege and ask my opinion, I would say: destroy all provincial printing houses with no mercy, create a monopoly for printing on the template of the existing tobacco monopoly." The mayor spoke in the voice of an ultra-royalist: the shepherd should save his flock from the plague of the press free of censorship. That ultra-royalist truly believed that such a step would be significant on the road toward a France "cleansed of the Jacobin dirt."

"Jacobins"—that was the buzzword. And so was called everyone who favorably mentioned the Declaration of the Rights of Man or a victorious battle at Wagram. A "Jacobin" was anyone who dared state a slightly liberal opinion that would be a shade different from the system of political beliefs of the ultra-royalists. Fear and hypocrisy reigned supreme. The common saying then was that a man was given speech in order to hide his thoughts, which is not necessarily an innovative statement but characterizes well the social climate of the Restoration. Julien Sorel remembered that maxim—after all, it made hypocrisy the wisdom of the era. Hypocrisy is always an offspring of humiliation, fear, and hopelessness. Hypocrisy, at times, also happens to be the path to a brilliant career realized through intrigue and a lack of scruples. Yet being in the presence of hypocrisy is always humiliating and infuriating. For

how could one react differently when watching Napoleonic generals who sold themselves to the Bourbons
and bowed and scraped hypocritically just to gain admission to the aristocratic salons? How did one react
when those people silently and full of humiliation
suffered slandering of the Napoleonic legend? Nevertheless, it was a necessary condition to succeed in the
Restoration era. No wonder then that every single day
taught hypocrisy to Lucien Leuwen or Julien Sorel,
those naive admirers of truth in the world that was
living a shameless lie.

V

There is a town. And in it was a clever Monsieur Valenod, from *The Red and the Black*, who was "characterized by impudence and boorishness. Since 1815, since
the return of the Bourbons his triumphant career only
strengthened those wonderful virtues. He ruled in
Verrières . . . never sporting a blush, meddling in everything, running, writing, talking incessantly, devoid of
personal dignity. . . . Valenod said once to the local
commoners: 'Give me the two stupidest from among
you;' to the clerks: 'Show me two of the greatest ignora-
muses;' and to the doctors: 'Fetch me the two greatest

charlatans.' Having thus gathered the shabbiest of every profession, he said: 'Let's rule together!'"

In a fragment of a broken mirror the whole world can be seen—a small town reflects a whole country. The mechanism of degeneration of a corruptible country and the junction between the world of politics and money—all that is as visible as bacteria under a microscope. Therefore, local press and the sovereign public opinion pose a natural threat to the corrupt relations. As observed by Stendhal, that is why local newspapers are being destroyed, civil liberties rationed, and journalists intimidated or corrupted.

How to get out of the town? Julien Sorel tried through the seminary. He kept repeating to himself: under Napoleon, I would have been a sergeant while amongst the future parish priests I will be a great vicar. He studied diligently the dogma and history of the Church and was a top student. However, instead of admiration he experienced only envy from others. The seminary teemed with informers and the students were instigated to engage in spying and denunciations. Diligence in studies was simply evidence of "sinful pride."

Stendhal was convinced that the Catholic Church was a hotbed of hypocrisy and an institution desiring an alliance between the altar and the throne, as well as the enemy of freedom and the spirit of Enlightenment. He refused to see in the Church the dealer of mercy and goodness; he chose not to remember the victims of the Jacobin terror. Moreover, he did not want to comprehend the tension present within the Church—between bearing witness and diplomacy, between the sacred and the profane, between the martyrdom of some and the benefits and hypocrisy of others. He came from the era in which a sea of blood was shed for the greatness of France, but according to Alfred de Musset, "Never was there such pure sunlight as that which dried all this blood." They said then that God sent the sunlight for Napoleon, "and they called it the Sun of Austerlitz."[6] At Napoleon's coronation ceremony, the pope blessed him and wanted to put a diadem on his head, adds Musset, but Napoleon took it out of his hands. It was then that an atheist reached for the watch and gave God a quarter hour to be struck with a thunderbolt.

The persistent drive of the men of the Church to retrieve all material possessions and political privileges once the Bourbons returned, their fear of freedom and modernity, and their demands for censorship and prosecution—all that composed a picture of an institution hostile to the revolution seeking freedom but conciliatory and helpless when facing the temptation of power and money.

Stendhal was highly venomous in his criticism of the Church. At the time of Voltaire—he said—the Church grasped that books were its true enemy. What are parliamentary debates? According to the clerics described by Stendhal, they are in reality nothing but mistrust and personal inquiries, which plants a bad habit of distrust in the hearts of the people. And that is highly suspicious—it questions everything, leads to independent judgments and triggers sinful curiosity. All triumphs in the sciences are deeply suspicious, for they harm the modesty of the heart and support the godless mind. Who is to stop the outstanding intelligentsia from joining the opposing camp, like the priests Sieyès or Grégoire have done? The pope remained the last reserve and the last hope. Only the pope could paralyze the spirit of criticism.

Hence, the good, honest, and evangelical priest is always poor and rejected, according to Stendhal, whereas a success-bound Catholic clergyman always sported goodness and sweetness on his face, which disappeared when business came into play. Then his countenance presented a "cunning combined with deep hypocrisy," "cold egoism of a priest sated with power and indulgence," while the "hope and ambition made him tremble with nervous anticipation."

## VI

The France of tradition and the France of revolution, the France of the Bourbons and the France of Napoleon . . .

These were indeed two kinds of France; these were two completely separate worlds that did not comprehend one another and simply hated one another. Stendhal spoke on behalf of the France devastated by the victory of hypocrites. Stendhal, a Napoleonic soldier and a lover of free thought, was watching the aristocratic salon of the Restoration with an ironic smile. These salons!—all's well if one does not make fun of God, the king, the priests, the influential dignitaries, and the artists promoted by the court, or anything that is accepted. All's well, providing one does snort at the praise for dissident poets and jeerers or for opposition newspapers, or Voltaire, Rousseau, or anything that might smack of slightly independent thought. And no talking politics . . . Apart from the previously mentioned, it was acceptable to talk about everything.

All the dirty tricks were going on behind the scenes.
Julien Sorel, while watching the salons and the back-
rooms, slowly understood: if I wish to climb higher, I
must learn all these lies and dirty tricks, and master
to cover them with sentimental clichés. He had no
illusions—it was necessary to reject all scruples and
extinguish even the smallest "spark of nobility." He repeated, "I, a plebeian, thrown down by rotten luck to
the lowest rank, I whom that luck gave a noble heart
and denied at least a thousand francs of allowance, that
is, strictly speaking, denying me bread, then why should
I reject the pleasure coming my way? My word, I am
not stupid! Let everyone take care of himself in the desert of egoism called life." He soon learned how to take
care of his interests in that "desert of egoism." He
learned how to praise what one disparages in one's
heart, and how to condemn what one loves deep inside.
He learned to lie so well and reached such mastery in
the servile newspeak that he astounded his listeners,
who perceived in him "a greater Jesuit than they were
themselves." At times, he was disgusted with the sound
of his own voice as he sensed something filthy in that
speech that stank of stolen money.

VII

The sad order of the Restoration was a compromise between nostalgia for freedom, for the glory of the Jacobins, the Republicans, the Bonapartists, and the radicalism of the Ultras seized with their mad belief in counterrevolution—that is, the return to the former prerevolutionary world. Even in Louis XVIII the Ultras saw another personification of succumbing to Jacobinism, and for them the Restoration was but a facade behind which the people of the revolution and their customs hid.

The Ultras identified their enemy with no trouble—it was the liberals. One of the Ultras wrote: "It is these ambitious swine that changed the shirt of a ploughman into the coat of a townie and in this disguise seek in the industry and commerce the means which would allow them to denounce the names of their fathers, as they have already rejected their virtues. It is these pedantic students, vain, insolent, and unruly, the great waves of whose the university and thousands of high schools flood France with. It is these buffoon politicians, debating, judging, and pontificating, out of whom many can even read, well to a reasonable degree. . . . It is also this impoverished nobility, who most of all and by all means wishes to have money and then more money because if one has money, one can get by without honor, so if the need be, they might make noble even their infamy" (Jose Cabanis, *Charles X: The King of Ultras*).

The passion and contempt of the aristocrat who watches his class losing France to the bourgeoisie goes well with the passion and disdain of Stendhal, an aristocrat by spirit and a liberal by beliefs. Here is the salon of the Restoration era and the guests, the richest people in Paris. Many of them grew up in poverty and were once workers or artisans. Now, one of them is a rich factory owner and a deputy. Right next to him there is a cheerful blockhead of incredible dullness who happens to be a champion of the stock exchange and is unable to utter a single reasonable sentence. We also see a famous writer, the master of salon conversations. This time, however, busy with jockeying for the seat at the Academy of Literature, our man of letters will be afraid to harm his interests by malicious jokes about eminent personages. Therefore he remains silent.

And here is the richest factory owner in his industry, a true go-getter. Ten years ago he was a common worker, but owing to two faked bankruptcies he became a millionaire. And here we have a captain of the Parisian national guard, owner of a few factories supported by the government. Another one, a general bearing a famous historical name, has a beautiful landed property for sale. He used to be an ambassador but was excessively two-faced even for a diplomat. Once he disgraced his office, he was let go, so he switched to business and started buying company shares. Finally, here is the wealthiest landowner in Burgundy who pays the highest taxes. He accompanies his mother and goes to mass every Sunday. He borrows two sous from his mother to pay for the church seat. "I am certain," writes Stendhal, "that he never pays her back." And the salon conversations? It is the boredom of life filled exclusively with ambition and representation, with no participation of the heart.

We know those salons and those conversations. They are immortal—they have survived cataclysms and wars, revolutions and dictatorships, in order to enter our times victoriously. Boredom and cynicism are the natural progeny of salons from which thought, honesty, and authenticity were escorted out. The ubiquitous boredom is a characteristic of close-up milieus, self-blocked spirituality, impotence in the dialogue for a changing world, and saturated with resentment toward what is unfamiliar and new. Boredom means gossip instead of information, intrigue instead of debate, and a pitiful parade of careerists instead of politicians concerned about the common well-being. Boredom triumphs when the reality is perceived as constant and not worthy of change. Then reality appears as a carousel of human mannequins and a world devoid of ideas in which careerists write their fate with Vaseline while the rejected and the defeated do with bile. Such a world indeed is a "desert of egoism."

However, the world is not always as we people make it out to be. After all, even in the worst of the worlds we may still live according to our values; even in the midst of oppression and indignity it is possible to reject the opportunism of ritualistic gestures. It requires only a pinch of imagination and a dollop of consistency. It might also call for a bit of courage and quite a bit of patience, as even the longest night is followed by a dawn.

Stendhal was mad at the boredom of the Restoration drawing rooms, both the aristocratic and the *nouveau riche*. Nevertheless, he was still capable of creating his own world that was not all about boredom, ambition, and representation. It was the world of his books. Stendhal may have been bored at a drawing room, but I am not bored when reading *The Charterhouse of Parma;* Stendhal may have been bored with a count or a banker, but I am not at all bored by Julien Sorel or Lucien Leuwen. It is people who create boredom, so people can also break it up. One may leave a drawing room, one may leave the clichés, and one may leave the insatiable drive to climb the social ladder—and simply go for a walk with Stendhal.

The picture of progressing degradation in the elites is disgusting, when the people with the original ideas leave and the people scrambling up the career ladder arrive, and when better money is daily driven out by worse money—it is then exactly when one may choose the moral comfort over the material one. Participation in the rat race is not mandatory. Money need not necessarily be worshiped. A careerist with no moral backbone does not have to be a role model for everybody. Certainly, they were not models for Stendhal. He stated: I despise offices. And he warned: You shall perish if you do not take it upon yourself to be honest. He had a motto: Frankness and honesty. It may sound a bit exalted, the more so as Stendhal was known to be whimsical and inconsistent. That democrat by belief and aristocrat by heart could not stand the *nouveau riche* with a passion comparable to the contempt exhibited by the ultra-aristocrats.

He was a defender of the regime and at the same time an adorer of freedom. These two are not mutually exclusive, and therefore it does not preclude the people raised to the top by the Restoration. A legitimist despises them because they are of low birth, exhibit base behavior, and they do not respect chivalry or the tradition. Stendhal despised them because they exchanged the call to freedom, equality, and fraternity for the motto "Get rich!" The latter was the true credo of the contemporary liberals who wished to assume power, and such was the appearance of the ideas of liberty translated into the language of money and tough market competition.

## VIII

Stendhal considered himself a liberal, at least at the time of their squabbles with the ultras and "the clerical party." "I am from their party," he said. In practice, it meant that just like the liberals he supported freedom in everything—in religion and philosophy, in scientific research and literature, in economy and political life. Just like liberals, Stendhal was an heir to the Enlightenment, a lover of reason and the Enlightenment style of jokes, sarcasm, and irony. Above all, he was a writer and an observer of his time, and not an ideologue or a politician. He looked at things in a different way. Liberals built their identity on a double protest, one against the despotism of absolute monarchs, and the other against the despotism of the revolutionary mob. This also included the despotism of Napoleon. And Stendhal loved Napoleon . . .

Liberal critique stigmatized both Jacobin terror and any despotism of the rule of the majority that suppressed the rights of the minority. Liberals maintained that once the epoch of the revolution and Napoleonic wars was over—which they considered "a historical nonsense"—there came a time of commerce and industry, credit and free competition, and the era of peace. Therefore, liberals were unfriendly toward the Republican ideals, in which they perceived a hidden temptation for the autocracy of people, understood the Jacobin way, or simply for a revolutionary dictatorship. They preferred an order of the constitutional monarchy and a Montesquieuan division of powers. Instead of universal suffrage and referendums, they preferred limited elections defined by material standing, justified by the "ignorance of the masses" that could be easily manipulated by the legitimists.

Liberals honestly hated the *ancien régime;* they viciously attacked the Church and political clericalism but at the same time condemned revolutionary terror. They felt themselves a minority loosely ingrained in the French tradition. They were in a way exclusive, hence willing to strike a compromise with every authority—from Napoleon through the Bourbons to the regime of Louis-Philippe. That is why they saw no end to the accusations of their weak character, cowardice, and careerism. When characterizing Benjamin Constant, the most eminent liberal intellectual, a contemporary politician of the right wing wrote: "In the case of Constant, as often happens among the liberals, the power of conviction stands in an amazing contrast to the weakness of character. Didn't he use what was best in him in his writings, and what was worse in his life?" (Dominique de Villepin, *One Hundred Days*).

Stendhal described life. He respected liberal values but usually despised the politicians of the liberal camp. He would say Mr. D. was a brave liberal, arch-moral prefect, the man of best intentions, heroic and "the stupidest of the liberal writers." He would also say: all those ultraliberals are very respectful of their immaculate virtue but apart from that are unable to comprehend that two and two is four. What angered him with the liberals were "heaviness, slowness, and virtue afraid of the smallest truth," "the lack of any notion stretching out of mediocrity," and, in a sign of the times, the venality toward the new governments after 1830. "A notorious good-for-nothing sold himself in 1841," "the cheekiest liar of the vilest physiognomy," "the most puffed-up and ceremonious of my compatriots," two brothers of "big Jesuit faces with a fake and cross-eyed glance"—these are the expressions used by Stendhal when he wrote about the liberals.

In the meantime, a certain conservative count, universally respected and considered one the greatest minds of his era, would say jeeringly: "I am sovereign. Why demand of me to hold the same views as six weeks ago? In that case, principles would be my tyrant." And that reminds me of a certain politician who held the office of prime minister for a quarter century. When asked by journalists if it is a normal country in which the prime minister does not change, he would answer,

truly amazed: "What?! You mean I don't change?"
Somewhat cynical, I would say . . .

We know various kinds of cynicism. We know the
cynicism of an opportunist greedy for power and money, but we also know the cynicism of sober and insightful critics. The former was the attribute of the count
and the prime minister, while the latter characterized
Stendhal. The writer, having to pick between a virtuous
moron and a depraved cynic, would simply choose the
charterhouse of Parma.

## IX

He could be unjust, and admitted to it many a time.
After all, the world of politics is not composed of
moralists and intellectuals. That world is ruled by
astuteness, cunning, the sense of compromise and intrigue. Truth, spiritual depth, and honor are not exactly
the attributes of parliamentary politics. However, the
question is if politics are actually motivated by any set
of values higher and nobler than a struggle for power
and money, and a game of ambition and jealousy?
Stendhal perceived the politics of the Restoration period and the July monarchy as vanity and villainy fairs.
What is the parliament if not a great fair, where every-

one peddles his conscience, or what is considered a conscience, selling it in exchange for an office or a position? These words were written by the Catholic priest Félicité Robert de Lamennais, but just as easily Stendhal could have written them. The logic of the free-market economy became transferred to the world of politics, including the parliament. Ideas were of no value any longer; what counted only were demand and supply, the stocks and profit.

That whole world was repulsive to Stendhal. He was looking at it with an eye of a writer who remembered the pathos of not long ago—the greatness of Napoleon. Now it was only the numb and mendacious ultra royalists supported by depraved priests, saturated with a bizarre combination of fanaticism and hypocrisy. On the other hand, there were corrupt, cynical *parvenus* who waved the three-color flag of the revolution in order to secure a job in the administration or a government contract. The former praised the tradition but cared exclusively about their power and landed properties while shaking in their boots for fear of a new revolution. The latter, while advocating rights of man, in reality believed only in the law of money. The great dispute between tradition and revolution, between the spirit of Christendom and the spirit of Enlightenment, between the aristocratic ethos and the republican ethos, between Chateaubriand and Napoleon, turned into a brawl of a fanatical Catholic hypocrite with a venal liberal, a corrupt swine. A feud between "the Jesuit" and "the banker" for positions and money was what remained of the great ideals of Stendhal's youth.

It was the time of little and spiteful deeds and people. Everything became a commodity and everything was for sale. The July Revolution of 1830 brought a spell of hope. It finally dethroned the ultras and put Louis-Philippe in power. Soon, Stendhal called the new monarch "the greatest scoundrel among kings." Everything in him was shallow and corrupt. The ministers stole everything, following the example of their king. "The slogan *enrichissez-vous* (get rich) became a foundation on which the authority built its power," Andrzej Zahorski wrote. "The government in its majority was composed of paid-off mediocrities and various careerists. . . . The ministers kept stealing with extreme insolence. Scandals were so grandiose that it was impossible to cover them up and they scandalized, shocked or entertained the society. The minister of public works, the minister of war, and the minister of internal affairs found themselves among those well-known thieves of the public property."

"We are up to our ears in mud," wrote Stendhal in a letter to Prosper Mérimée.

Mérimée replied, "You are right and if not for my shyness, I would say: in s——."

X

Even when drowning in mud, every man needs some sort of authenticity, be it only for a while. Everybody looks for some kind of a secret weapon when fighting the ubiquitous mud, hoping this weapon will allow him to regain self-esteem.

Two romantic relationships with two unusual women were that secret weapon for Julien Sorel. Both women were from high society, and both were head over heels in love with the plebeian and ready to sacrifice everything for him. Both were also separated from Julien by an im-passable barrier of breeding and money. For his lovers he was everything, but for their world he was nothing. It was as if he lived in a crevasse between his feeling of his own individual value and an understanding of his complete lack of social value. When facing the court of law, he said these memorable words to the jury: "I do not have the privilege of belonging to your sphere; you see in me only a peasant who rebelled against the wickedness of his fate."

And then he added that the judges "through my person would like to punish and deter forever this class of the youth who was born in a low estate and stifled with poverty, but was lucky enough to have obtained the education and was audacious enough to squeeze into the sphere which the arrogance of the rich calls the world." Sorel's generation could only hopelessly curse the villainy of their fate. They were fully aware they were up to their ears in mud.

How to live in a world like this? To advance in a career, one had to accept the rules of the game. One had to choose hypocrisy over truth, opportunism over principles, cunning and intrigue over straightforwardness, and shallowness over greatness. One had to accept the fate of a nobody, prostitute one's ideals and principles, hopelessly bite the tongue and secretly clench the fist, pander to the fools and *canailles*, and start believing that hypocrisy, intrigue, and money would dictate everything forever. And only repeat: get rich, get rich, get rich!

However, that is not enough: accepting the divine mission of money and participating in the intrigues and villainy of the epoch, it was necessary also to turn one's

back to the world of those excluded, harmed, and degraded. And one had to tremble with fear awaiting the
moment when all those harmed and degraded would
set out toward another Bastille to shout out: "Enough!"

Yes, Stendhal was furious and his fury may easily
amaze. He was not a man of one great idea that would
order him to totally reject the Restoration, like the Ultras or Jacobins did. Moreover, that Restoration was so
velvety. . . . Louis XVIII renounced revenge on the
people of the revolution and the empire. A vast majority of Napoleonic officials kept their offices. Even those
that had voted for the beheading of Louis XVI were not
touched. Things changed after the One Hundred Days.
It was then that the acts of retaliation started—the legitimists exacted their revenge even on the French citizens faithful to the emperor. Mob murders, to which
the authorities turned a blind eye, were accompanied by
denunciations and arrests. Andrzej Zahorski writes that
there functioned kangaroo courts presided over by
"judges who were in reality executioners unworthy of
the title of a judge. . . . So there were official and unof-
ficial murders; the white bow of the dynasty was stained
with French blood. The Bourbons, when residing safely
abroad, protested vehemently against Robespierre's

cruelty, and now they proved that there was no difference between the White and the Jacobin terror."

That is all true, but the fundamental matters remained the same: the very same elite administered the country, which in 1814, as phrased by Benjamin Constant, "jumped from one branch to the other." Louis XVIII honored military promotions of the Napoleonic era, and to some degree respected the parliamentary representation and freedom of the press. After 1830, old conflicts did not matter at all: the old legitimism and Bonapartism lost their significance—it was about the here and now. Coal and metallurgical industries kept developing, steam machinery made its way to the factories, sugar factories were being modernized, great advances were made in transportation, and the railways were started. The cities grew, illiteracy was in decline, primary education was highly cared for, and higher education developed. Mass press appeared on the scene and became the voice of the public opinion. France was becoming normal.

## XI

Obviously, there were two sides of this coin. Freedom of the press, though declared publicly, was systematically suppressed as it brought to light the dirt and corruption scandals that the governments wanted to hide. When the official imperial repressions became too embarrassing, a process of corrupting the papers and journalists started. "The type of venal journalist, writing only to make money and often without conviction but for a lavish fee became widespread all over the country. People with a talent for writing were available and could be bought, and they prostituted their conscience unceremoniously, with no inhibition whatsoever. A new generation of journalists was growing, without any internal dilemmas or doubts," writes Zahorski. But didn't the corruption of the journalists appear in all democracies?

Let us imagine a young writer who wishes to debut in Paris. He believes his writing makes sense; he believes in the freedom of man and in his rights, and in the honor and greatness of France. As long as he was fighting the censorship that confiscated his writing, he understood the sense and value of his work. The enemy was clearly defined: despotism and censorship. But suddenly the censorship disappears. A new ruler emerges: a publisher-owner. What does our writer hear from him? This won't sell, please make it shorter by half as it is too long and boring. And simplify it because our reader will not grasp it; and change that sad ending because our readers will not like it.

Well, the readers were trouble. Papers and books became products and their fate depended on the market while the readership taste was shaped by the rich bourgeoisie. This bourgeoisie sought sensation, thrill, and entertainment in a paper or a book. Our writer grew to understand that he was expected to sell. And he heard the cynical confession from his publisher: I trade in words; your articles, read today, will be forgotten tomorrow. They are of no greater value to me than the price that was paid for them. He also heard: be clever and obedient, and learn to pander to the baseness of the literary clans—this is the secret for success.

This picture of the world of literature—as painted by its contemporaries—is obviously drawn with the exaggeration of a caricaturist. After all, it was a grand time in French literature, the time of Stendhal and Balzac, Hugo and Sainte-Beuve, Chateaubriand and Tocqueville. Nevertheless, it is worthwhile to listen to those angry observations. Who remembers the publishers of Stendhal or Balzac today, and if they do, then for what reason? If we keep them in grateful memory, it is only because they decided to publish the authors who today make up a great canon of French literature even though some of them did not bring quick profits. The publishers made the world look at France with respect and admiration. Paris owed them its status as the Mecca of European culture and an intellectual powerhouse, as well as its continued spiritual freedom.

Two philosophies clashed in that world of the Restoration. The Ultras demanded that the old, prerevolutionary order be restored so things could be "as they once were." This nostalgic royalism fed on the memories of damages sustained at the time of the revolution and the empire. These were the memories of the guillotine, confiscations, a harlot raised to the altar, treacherous murders, and the humiliation of many years of expulsion. The remembrance of damages sustained them; the Ultras wanted to go back to that river again—they wanted revenge. For them, noted Stendhal sneeringly, "there existed only two classes of people in France—the nobility, which was to be ruled with honor and rewarded with the blue ribbon, and the *canaille*, which was to be thrown a lot of sausage and ham at great occasions but which was to be hanged and massacred whenever it tried to raise a voice in protest."

"Only the feeling of jealousy," he wrote, "was able to enliven a little their dead hearts; no manifestations of nobleness or magnanimity are able to penetrate through their hardened spirit. They continue to live while led by the desire of some blind revenge. They are only stirred by the feelings of wickedness and baseness. The revolution of 1789 and Voltaire were not abominable to them; they simply never existed."

The attitude of moderate royalists was different. They understood it was impossible to cross the same river twice. Therefore, they tried to change everything in such a manner so it stayed the same. Such a viewpoint could easily be accepted by the society worn out by years of revolution and chaos, terror and fear, and wars won or lost but always bloody. So it was a philosophy of compromise that was to reconcile the victors with the losers, the tradition with the revolution. Such a compromise cannot have been fully successful. The heirs to the revolution wanted a republic, while the ultra royalists perceived that "rotten compromise" as the fruit of "the government of treason." One could say that such was the end of royalist illusions, and such was the end of the revolutionary illusions. The legitimism of the Ultras was equally utopian as the Jacobin republic of virtue.

For Stendhal—virulent in his anti-clericalism and contempt for the Ultras' hypocrisy—that "rotten compromise," triumphant particularly after July 1830, was a defeat suffered by all ideas: the republican and royalist, revolutionary and conservative, Catholic and Enlightenment alike. It was simply a complete triumph of money. The rest was but a masquerade.

## XII

Monsieur Leuwen Senior, a banker who became a deputy purely on a whim, has just overthrown another government by the strength of his own intrigue. However, he ponders the question:

> "What should I demand? If I don't assume one of the leading positions, the government, formed with my participation, will start mocking me and my situation will be ridiculous. Let's say they make me the general tax collector—I don't care for the monetary compensation connected with this office, and in view of my current influence in the parliament it would only be a mediocre success. I could make Lucien a prefect against his will. But then, I'd hand the weapon to a friend who becomes the minister of internal affairs. Within three months, he would push me into the mud by firing Lucien from his office."

"Don't you think you would be most admirable by doing a lot of good and not taking anything in exchange for it?" asked Mrs. Leuwen.

"Nobody's going to believe it. Monsieur de Lafayette has played that role for some forty years and he has always been just a step away from ridicule. Our society is too gangrenous to comprehend things like that. Three quarters of Paris would love Monsieur de Lafayette, if he stole some four million."

That is what Stendhal said. What a dream for men Monsieur de Lafayette would be if he were alive today . . .

Let us look at things through Stendhal's eyes: instead of democracy, money ruled; instead of a great idea, money; instead of quality and taste of life, money; instead of dignity, honor, and solidarity, money. Everything was for sale: a stage play's success, a mandate of the deputy, a position in the supervisory board, or a public office. And everybody could be bought: yesterday's count and yesterday's Jacobin, a politician and a banker, a lawyer and a journalist, a husband and a wife. The world of blue-blooded counts struck a secret pact with the world of ambiguously enriched *parvenus*, although the former and the latter declared to be sworn enemies on the outside.

Stendhal was suffocating in this world of sworn hypocrites, arrogant stock profiteers, and fattened champions of fraud who believed money decided their human value. It was the world of the ultimate market, the market with no human face. A historian of the epoch writes:

> An enterprise becomes a sovereign organism, driving to obtain its own interests and goals, led only by the laws of its own logic, a tyrant which changes anybody that encounters it into its own slave. A complete dedication to the enterprise, an absolute devotion to the entrepreneur in the interest of competitive capability, success and the company's expansion, its abstract, ruthless drive for success becomes terrifying and obsessed with the one intrusive thought. The system becomes independent of its representatives and transforms into a mechanism whose course cannot be stopped by any human power. ... As the means and foundations of economic success elude an individual, people grow more

uncertain and have a stronger feeling that they are completely subjected to the lawlessness of the monster. As soon as the business diversifies and interconnects, the fight becomes more heated and more desperate; the monster assumes more forms and the collapse seems more and more inevitable. Finally, the competitors loom everywhere, the opponents and enemies, everybody fights everybody, and everybody is on the front line of the ceaseless, comprehensive and truly "total" war. Every possession, every position and every influence has to be won anew on a daily basis; it has to be captured and exhorted; everything gives an impression that nothing is trustworthy or permanent. This is the source of overwhelming skepticism and universal pessimism, and hence the stifling fear of life. (Arnold Hauser, *The Social History of Art*)

This is what remained of freedom, equality, and fraternity, and of the glory and pride of Napoleon's victories.

"What sacred thing remained with us?" pondered Alfred de Vigny. "In the total defeat of beliefs, to what shreds can the noble heart cling to? Apart from the love of affluence and one-day luxury, nothing is visible on the edge of the precipice. One could think that the egoism drowned everything. . . . Today, leaders of the political parties take Catholicism for a slogan and a banner, but how do they believe in its miracles and how do they observe its principles in their own lives?"[7]

Where can one find spiritual support in order not to succumb to the spirit of the times? This support can be provided, writes de Vigny, "by the proud and unshakable feeling, the instinct of incomparable beauty. . . . This instinct is called *Honor*. . . . When honor comes into play, man feels that something was touched within him, something which constitutes a part of his being, and immediately all his pride and might awaken in him. . . . Honor is conscience, but multiplied. . . . It breeds charitable deeds which cannot be surpassed by the evangelical mercy; it is capable of wonderful tolerance, tender kindness, divine leniency and noble forgiveness. Always and everywhere does it sustain the human dignity in all its beauty."[8]

One could add the following to these lofty words: Honor is a brave, honest and uncompromising analysis of the world. It is a severe analysis, devoid of any perfunctory cautiousness. It is also the ability to say to the high and mighty of this world: *non serviam.*

Stendhal said, "One could be unhappy, but to lose honor?"

Nicolas Chamfort noted, "Nearly all people live in slavery for the reason the Spartans gave as the cause of the slavery of Persians: they are not able to utter the syllable 'no.' To be able to utter this word and to be able to live alone are the only two ways to preserve one's own freedom and identity."

## XIII

And to the question of "Will you be a true scoundrel?" I reply: "No, I will not."

# FIVE

# Canaille, Canaille, Canaille!

In memoriam
Kazimierz Brandys

I

In *The Red and the Black*, Stendhal described a ball. A wonderful ball. All eyes were fixed on Mathilde who came from one of the most famous families in France. People of this family looked down with contempt on this new era known as the Restoration. So what if they retrieved the properties confiscated by the Revolution? And what is so special about the fact that after several years of humiliations they returned to their palaces and assumed high offices in the country? It was no longer their state. This was not the state of the Condé and the Turenne, the country of victorious battles and great aristocratic romances, the balls and the hunting, and the passion and thrills.

Now everything had become boorish. The people who were in the mob storming the Bastille, who took the crown off the head of Louis XVI and then guillo-tined the monarch, who stomped on and kicked the Bourbon lilies while wearing the three-colored flags, and who started as butchers and cobblers, and ended as generals and margraves, who bought their count titles with money, who served the usurper, that "Corsican bandit," those people who humiliated and defiled the honor of France—these people populated the drawing rooms of Paris that day.

Mathilde despised the world of these people. She lived in the great history—in the history of France and her own family. For her, the most important day was April 30, 1574. On that day, Boniface de La Môle, the adored lover of Queen Marguerite of Navarre, was be-headed in the Place de Grève. "Those sixteenth-century Wars of the League," she said, "are France's era. . . . Everyone was fighting for something they wanted to

make their party triumphant, and not just to plodding-
ly earn a medal, the way they did in your emperor's
time. You'll surely agree there was less egoism, and less
pettiness. I love that time."[1] "To your emperor ..."
Mathilde used this contemptuous turn of phrase in the
conversation with Julien Sorel, a young man from the
lower classes who served her father as a clerk.

Julien Sorel was of peasant stock, from provincial
poverty. He tried to break out from his estate through a
religious seminary, unable to find any other way. Sorel
was taught about life by an old surgeon, a knight of the
Legion of Honor, who rented a room at Julien's parents'
house. The town's mayor, a careerist and an adorer of
the Restoration, thought the surgeon "might very well
have been, after all, a secret agent for the liberals. He
used to say that our mountains' air was good for his
asthma, but who knows if that was true or not? He was
with *Buonaparte* on all his Italian campaigns and once,
I've heard, he even voted against the Empire."[2] In a
word, the surgeon was a Jacobin who enlivened the
"passions of the small town, seething with hatred." The
Jacobin gave Julien *Memoirs of Napoleon on Saint-
Helena*, a cultlike book of the epoch. When he died, he
left his Legion of Honor medal to Julien.

For Julien, a plebeian child, the Legion of Honor, Napoleon, and the Revolution—that was the greatness of France. Napoleon was for him the symbol of the Revolution and the glory. And for Mathilde? Mathilde may have heard the disquisition by Chateaubriand, an aristocrat and writer, politician and monarchist, who described the moment when the Revolution transformed France into the empire: "The enriched revolutionaries began moving into the palaces sold in the suburb of Saint-Germain. As Jacobins became barons and counts, they talked only about the atrocities of 1793, the necessity of punishing the proletariat and curbing the excesses of the mob. Bonaparte brought Brutuses and Scaevolas to his police to lavish medals on them, to blotch them with titles, and to force them to betray their own views and defend the committed murders. A new generation was growing up, the one born of blood; from that time on, they were the ones to spill blood, but only of the other ones. On a daily basis, the republicans transformed into the people of the empire and the tyranny of all into the despotism of one man."[3]

Stendhal said about Napoleon: "The only man I ever loved."[4]

II

Napoleon was for Stendhal, an atheist and a libertine, the faith, the hope, and the love. It was Napoleon who marked that time of pride and glory. The time of great hope is followed by the great disappointment. The sadness of Restoration follows the euphoria of the Great Revolution and the magnificent empire, just like a hangover and nausea after a wonderful binging session. That is exactly what Stendhal was describing.

He was not a politician and despised politics. But he loved life and he loved freedom. And he loved France. As he loved freedom, so in spirit he was a republican and the republic was for him a child of the Revolution. He loved France, so he was fascinated by the great Napoleon in whom he wished to see the bearer of freedom, equality, and fraternity—even under the imperial scepter. Finally, he loved life. He drank it in with great passion and engaged in all the hopes and affairs of his time while describing them with his masterly pen.

The chief of police in Milan wrote in his official report to Vienna on Stendhal: "He has become known as a non-religious, amoral, and dangerous enemy of legitimacy, on extremely friendly terms with our liberals of the worst opinion." We also read there: "This foreigner, who at the time of the Bonaparte Empire, held the office of auditor in the Board of State, is known as the author of the infamous work titled *Rome, Naples and Florence by Monsieur de Stendhal*. In this work, he not only developed highly harmful political ideas, but with his slanderous words also brought colossal shame onto the people residing in this and other Italian provinces, and was even so impudent as to take a highly reprehensible stand against the Austrian government." On the decision of the Austrian authorities, Stendhal was expelled from Trieste. Later on, when he was a consul in Civitavecchia, a Vatican official pressed the French government to recall "this agent of the revolutionary propaganda immediately."

"The agent of the revolutionary propaganda," I write this phrase again, enchanted with the stylistic beauty of it. What a harmonious literary form that is! Clearly, a police denunciation is an everlasting literary genre and an irremovable cultural component of every single epoch . . .

Giuseppe Tomasi di Lampedusa said about Stendhal that all the ideas he professed made him loathsome to the governments of the Restoration: "He was a libertine, a republican, a Bonapartist, and an anti-clerical. These four attitudes were very reprehensible until 1830, though they were not cohesive."[5]

Stendhal wrote about himself: "I am a democrat by nature and an aristocrat by custom; I would gladly give away my property and life to the people, as long as I need not meet with the rabble." And Stendhal's biographer added: "He belonged to those who want to profess truth and be on the side of righteousness but just like Montaigne or Montesquieu he did not desire martyrdom." That is true, but what is so strange or inappropriate in the fact that he preferred to attend the balls rather than stand in front of the execution squad?

### III

At this magnificent ball, alongside Mathilde and Julien, there was also Count Altamira, a Neapolitan, a liberal sentenced to death in his homeland, and also a devout Catholic, or a "bigot," as labeled by Sorel. This strange incongruity, religion wedded to a love of freedom, impressed him. For Sorel believed that the idea of most use to tyrants was that of God. For Altamira, the notion of God was key to human freedom. In other words, Sorel honestly hated the world because it was a world full of enslavement; Altamira somewhat naively loved the world because it was a world full of freedom.

Sorel provocatively approached Altamira by saying: "Danton was a *man!*"⁶ Mathilde, fascinated by the plebeian mysteriousness of Julien, asked in a tone of aristocratic disrespect: "Wasn't Danton a butcher?" To which Julien retorted: "Yes, as far as certain people are concerned.... But unfortunately for the aristocracy, he was in fact a lawyer. ... In other words, he began life like several of the Peers whom I see here this evening."⁷

Danton's name resounded ominously in the drawing rooms of the Restoration; it was one of the symbols of the Revolution. For some it was the symbol of radiant hope; for others, of unspeakable terror. The hope was embodied in the Declaration of the Rights of Man; the terror was embodied in the horrors of the guillotine, which eventually severed Danton's head.

Altamira was not a man of the guillotine. He was a participant in a recent "unsuccessful, ridiculous and preposterous plot," as sarcastically described by a certain margrave of a historical name. Count Altamira was a man of the cause and thought nothing so worthy of his attention as something, anything, that could bring bicameral legislative government to his country.

Despairing of Europe, poor Altamira had been reduced to imagining that, when the United States of South America grew large and powerful, they would be able to give Europe back the liberty that Mirabeau, and the French Revolution had given it.[8]

Toward the end of the ball, Julien turned to Altamira and said: "What a gorgeous ball! . . . There's nothing missing."

"Except thought," responded Altamira.[9]

Was Altamira right? He explained to Julien: "But in these drawing rooms, thought is utterly hateful. They don't dare rise above the level of a vaudeville song: that's what pays, here. But a thinking man, if his insights are forceful and original, gets labeled a cynic."[10]

Shallow canailles, despicable flatterers, boorishness and stupidity, filthy beasts—such are the epithets flung by Stendhal at the former republicans and Bonapartists who turned into the menials of the Restoration in *The Life of Henry Brulard*, which he wrote without any thought of publication.

It was then that the word "homeland" was degraded and humiliated. After all, "high treason" was the most heinous of all crimes for Stendhal.

## IV

In 1793, in the central square of Grenoble, two priests were beheaded. Many years later, Stendhal admitted that these deaths gave him pleasure. These words were shocking! Stendhal, a man of terror?! For him the revolutions meant freedom and tolerance. It was Mirabeau and Lafayette, and *not* Robespierre and the guillotine. But he could not tolerate the Jacobins. They seemed to him awfully ordinary. And he confessed: "I have this revulsion toward everything that is dirty, or damp, or blackish. I saw many of those things with those Jacobins." Where does this amazing confession come from? It comes from the revulsion toward the times and people of the Restoration. In the cruelty of the Jacobins, there was some brutal truth of patriotism.

And what of their enemies?

When a confessor tried to convince the young Beyle to respect the martyr priests, he answered the terrified priest impertinently:

"Grandpa told me that two protestant pastors were hanged in the same place twenty years ago."

"Oh, but that was completely different!

"Yes, the court sentenced the pastors for religion, while the court sentenced the priests for high treason."

"I didn't know then yet," adds Stendhal, "that it is dangerous to debate with tyrants; they must have read the lack of sympathy for the two traitors of the homeland in my eyes. (No, there was not a crime in 1795, and to my mind still there is none in 1835, even remotely comparable to that one.)"

No, Stendhal did not long for the Jacobin terror, but his contrary nature told him to side with the Jacobins and the homeland, and against those who assumed power in Paris, arriving "in foreign wagons."

"Homeland in danger"—what a new sense the Revolution gave to this battle cry! Homeland stopped being a property and a privilege of the monarchs and cardinals, the dukes and marshals. It became the property of the people—cobblers and tailors, sergeants and butchers. It became a common property for those who stormed the Bastille and who "of natural rights took the endowments," and advanced from a corporal to a general in Napoleon's army.

The Restoration? The Restoration meant the power of those who abandoned and betrayed the homeland, and supported the enemies of the motherland in order to return to Paris brought by the Prussian, British, or Russian bayonets. When the troops of the Revolution fought foreign armies, reminisces Stendhal, "I experienced the liveliest emotions of love to the motherland and hatred toward 'the aristocrats' (legitimists of 1835) and to the priests, her enemies."

Such was the situation in the years of the revolutionary wars. In the epoch of the Restoration, a patriotic slogan became a muzzle for the critically thinking or a springboard for a career in administration or the army. Stendhal scornfully termed this kind of life strategy "antechamber patriotism." "Trust me, Monsieur," he said, "all the patriots who sermonize so much about national honor are well paid!"

It must have been a curious kind of "patriotism" that forbade the possession of *Memoirs of Napoleon on Saint-Helena* and required the slander of Napoleon. This "antechamber patriotism" was simply hypocrisy so typical of the Restoration. Well, it was also a source of frustration for Julien Sorel.

V

Stendhal held his own opinions but avoided engagement in politics. His biographer later said that he always exhibited an ability to adjust to the circumstances, which characterizes an indifferent observer who is adamant about never getting excited. Jose Cabanis, author of an excellent biography of the king of the Ultras, Charles X, went even further. He said that Stendhal expressed his hatred toward the Church only in anonymous articles printed abroad or in the self-censored letters. He had no courage, and remained behind scenes of the opposition against the "priestly party," which would have found in him a valid adversary. In 1830, when *The Red and the Black* appeared, in which the "police chief of the Congregation" is shown as a man not avoiding murder, Bourbons were already abolished and Stendhal was a consul of the new regime. He profited from their defeat, though he did not contribute to it.

The scathing reasoning of Cabanis has a major flaw: Stendhal never maintained he was in the forefront of the fighters against the Restoration. So what that he wrote under a pseudonym? Or that he was cautious? How many writers—before and after him—did exactly the same? After all, it is better to stigmatize the unbearable regime under a pseudonym than pander to it under your own. He preferred to write about Rossini rather than about the ministers of the Restoration. What is so strange with that? Who wouldn't prefer to write about Stendhal rather than so-and-so?

Let us repeat: Stendhal was not a politician or an ideologue. The Restoration regime disgusted him for aesthetic and moral reasons. Lampedusa says that he was "a sensitive man, with a soul easily hurt, who reacted to outside stimuli by suffering but he also masked his vulnerability to trauma by cynicism and fanfaronade in public life; the writer wore his masks so well that he was able to fool even his closest friends."

What about the Bonapartism of Stendhal? Lampedusa would say that "Stendhal never had much liking to Napoleon the despot . . . he could not stand him . . . because he was a republican. . . . At the same time he adored him because he saw 'the master of energy' in him, and he truly admired his administrative methods which he knew so well."

So that is what Lampedusa had to say. As for the republicanism of Stendhal, well, that is a moot point. In a nutshell: at the time of the monarchy he was a republican; in the republic he would have adored the king. He had the ever-present spirit of critical observation, polemics, and contrariness. Maybe that is why he created his masterpieces?

To put it differently: Why do we love Stendhal? We do not love him for his heroism, as he never was an indomitable conspirator for freedom or a martyr of any "right cause." On the contrary, he shined in the Paris drawing rooms whose boredom he described with great venom; he held public offices although he felt diminished by the lack of appreciation for his own intelligence and former services; at the time of the domination of the "priestly party" he would say sacrilegious things like "God can be excused because he does not exist"—but that never brought any harm upon him. So he was neither a martyr nor a hero. He was a smart skeptic of insightful intelligence; he was wise with his wonderful irony and helpless anger. He was able to ridicule mercilessly because he could read the mysteries of the human soul.

Therefore, we love Stendhal, this expert in pandering, for his lack of hypocrisy, for honesty toward himself, for dignity when confronted with villainy, and for the sense of intrinsic value devoid of narcissism and devastating megalomania. His political helplessness transformed into a general fury when he painted the picture of the Restoration and the gallery of characters of that peculiar era, when the characters collapsed and human souls degraded but France kept growing more powerful and people grew richer every month.

Obviously, not everyone grew richer. There were those who still lived in poverty. Stendhal was sincere in his solidarity with the people and he just as sincerely despised the mob. In other words: he adored and respected the people who abolished the Bastille and engaged in a fight for freedom and civic rights. However, when the fight for freedom turned into a ruthless drive for power and merciless revenge, the people became a mob. Freedom, equality, and fraternity changed then into their opposites: terror, enslavement, and cruelty. "Be my brother or else I shall kill you," said the Jacobins. And kill they did.

Benjamin Constant, witness of that epoch, wrote: "In all violent fights, interests follow the trace of the declared opinions like vultures would the troops ready for battle. Hatred, vindictiveness, greed, and ingratitude cheekily parody the noblest models because they were asked to be imitated in such an inept way. A perfidious friend, a dishonest debtor, a shady informer, and a venal judge will find in advance their apology in a conventional language. Patriotism becomes a trivial excuse for every crime." Stendhal understood this mechanism only too well.

François Mauriac, a Catholic adversary of Stendhal's in the twentieth century, wrote: "This incomparable painter of many a crazy soul has avoided exaggeration both in art and in life. The admirer of many spectacular crimes, he was incapable of any other excesses but the verbal ones. The sense of moderation kept him from a bad romantic taste but it did not save him from playing the role of a ghastly man in the drawing rooms, from whose stories ladies flee in panic. . . . There is not a trace of wickedness in Stendhal." Perhaps that is also why we love Stendhal?

VI

Let us return to the ball and the conversation between Count Altamira and Julien Sorel. Says Altamira:

"Note that, in the revolution which I found myself leading, we failed only because I refused to have three heads cut off, and I would not distribute to our supporters seven or eight millions, deposited in a box to which I had the key. My king, who today is burning to grab me, and who before the revolt had been on the first-name terms with me, would have given me the greatest medal in the land, had I cut off those three heads and handed out the money, because then I would have been at least half successful, and my country would have had a sort of constitution. . . . That's how the world works, it's all a chess game."

"But then," responded Julien, his eyes blazing, "you didn't know how to play. Now . . ."

"You mean, now I'd cut off those heads, and I wouldn't be the Girondin you made me out to be the other day? . . . I'll answer you," said Altamira sadly, "after you've killed a man in a duel, which is at least not so ugly as having him killed by an executioner."

"My Lord!" said Julien. "The man who desires a goal, also desires the way of accomplishing it. If I had any power, instead of being, as I am, a mere atom, I'd have three men killed if I could save the lives of four."

His glance glowed with moral fire, and with contempt for men's senseless decisions.[11]

This dialogue is in reality Stendhal talking to himself. It is also a portion of the never-ending debate of people of the revolutionary and Napoleonic generation who cannot find their place in the new era. The time of heroism has passed and the past ideals became only a troublesome decoration of the real life. The heroes of yesterday must leave to make room for profiteers and rogues. The world of values gives way to the world of effectiveness.

Altamira was a liberal who headed the revolution against despotism or the revolution in the name of freedom. A revolution is an act of violence that, in the eyes of the liberal dating to the prerevolutionary era, or a time of former principles, may be justified only by the immediate abandonment of violence once the victory is secured. Therefore Altamira, just like Lafayette, did not cut off his enemies' heads; he rejected violence; he did not want to kill. That is why he lost.

Julien Sorel, however, is not an aristocrat and a liberal who rejected despotism and chose freedom. Sorel is a plebeian who loves the revolution and Napoleon just because they had their enemies beheaded. He thinks differently from Altamira. He knows that in the Napoleonic era he, "who was not born a lackey," would have been a colonel before the age of thirty, and later a general of Napoleon's army. The emperor is truly his ideal. Sorel admires the "Little Corporal" for his talent of a *parvenu*, for his will of advancement from the lower classes, who brings glory to France and becomes the ruler of the world. He also admires Napoleon for his ruthlessness in realizing these goals.

That prince of the fables promised greatness while the Restoration sentenced Julien to shabby vegetation amongst careerism and hypocrisy. The chances created for the likes of Julien by the Revolution were cancelled by the Restoration. Energy and talent, diligence and courage—these were (until recently) tickets to success in history for the poor and those of low birth. The Restoration reserved everything for the old nobility and the new plutocracy.

Julien is pondering the question whether it is permissible, when faced with this blatant injustice, to reach for contemptible means like lies, hypocrisy, and violence. "In fact," he told himself, after meditating a long time, "if these Spanish liberals had compromised the people's cause by committing crimes, they would not have been so easily swept away. These were arrogant children, and mere talkers . . . like me!" he suddenly exclaimed, as if waking with a start. "What difficult things have I ever done, to give myself the right to judge these poor devils, who in the end, once in their lifetimes, actually dared, actually started to *act*? . . . Who knows how you'll deal with some grand deed, once it's under way?"[12]

Stendhal observed: "I confess that the weakness that Julien demonstrates, in this monologue, gives me a poor opinion of him. He'd be worthy of joining ranks with those parlor liberals, in their yellow gloves, who convince themselves they're changing the whole way of life in a great country, but who can't possibly have on their consciences the tiniest, most harmless scratch."[13] So says Stendhal the Jacobin. And Julien stands "admiring the great qualities of Danton, Mirabeau, and Carnot, who had known how to escape defeat."[14]

Julien meditates: "A revolution cancels all a capricious society's titles and distinctions. In a revolution, a man assumes whatever rank he earns by his behavior in the face of death. . . . What would Danton be today . . .? Not even a deputy attorney general . . . What am I talking about? He'd be a government minister, because the great Danton, after all, did his share of stealing. Mirabeau sold himself, too. Napoleon stole millions, in Italy, and without that wealth, poverty would have stopped him in his tracks. . . . Only Lafayette never stole. Is stealing required? Is selling yourself inevitable?"[15] "Was Danton right to steal? . . . Should the revolutionaries of Piedmont, of Spain, have committed the crimes that compromised the people? Should they have given even totally unworthy people all the commissions in the army, and all the medals? Wouldn't the people wearing these medals have worried that the king might retake his throne? Should they have let the hordes loose, on the treasures of Turin? In short, . . . must the man who wants to eliminate ignorance and crime from the earth—must he sweep across the earth like a hurricane and do evil however it happens to take place?"[16]

These are the dilemmas of Julien's epoch. Can crime be annihilated with another crime? Or does inevitably that crime breed another crime?

## VII

One might think that a change from Jacobin terror and Napoleon's wars to peace, though filled with intrigue, hypocrisy, and money, is not a bad exchange; in fact, it seems to be an obvious change for the better. After all, isn't it better to live and slowly get rich than fear the guillotine or die at the Berezina? Well, isn't it?

Agreed, but not in the case of Julien Sorel. His life experience was different. Julien never shook in his boots fearing the guillotine and did not fight death when retreating from Moscow with Napoleon's troops. For Julien, as for Karl Marx, the guillotine was a "strike of the hammer, which will obliterate all feudal ruins." Napoleon's wars were for him simply "a road to pride and glory."

Julien is led by fury. It is the fury of Stendhal's hopelessness and the fury of a plebeian grudge. This grudge, compounded by unfulfilled ambitions, gives birth to a hateful resentment of the world populated by the people of auspicious beginnings and ample riches, the world of those successful in life. Sorel perceived this world as a conspiracy against himself, and that is why he challenged this world. His grudge is not unlike a self-poisoning with the virus of jealousy. Envy may lead to a career achieved unscrupulously or a rebellion with abandon. The Restoration bred one and the other.

Victor Cousin, a philosopher of that era, created a philosophical system for the careerist. According to this philosophy, wrote Adam Sikora, "the victor is always right because he is the tool realizing the plan of the Providence." Hence, it is necessary to reject the barren sympathy toward the defeated. One needs to, wrote Cousin, "declare one's intention of joining the victorious party because it offers morality, civilization ... and the future, while the party of the defeated represents only the past."[17]

Such was the theory. The practice, however, was embodied in the conviction that the Restoration system, particularly in the epoch of Louis-Philippe, was ideal and that any attempt at improving it was harmful and stupid. Such was the belief of François Guizot, a historian and politician, prime minister of the government, a man in the opinion of Andrzej Zahorski "open-minded and personally honest." Zahorski writes: "Guizot drew his overly brutal conclusions from his knowledge of history. He deeply believed in the human illicitness and thought that everyone could be bought, while the difficulties were only a matter of the price to be paid." The insightful Lampedusa noted that the July revolution of 1830 brought to power precisely such a caliber of people: "take Thiers (the premier in 1836) who was a kind of Julien Sorel, but a Julien who refrained from the final shooting."

However, bitterness did not stop Julien from "the final shooting." The bitterness gave birth to the rebellion, which hit blindly. All of the French nineteenth century was a history of the grudge born of the bitterness of the Restoration, the era of the great disappointment, when grand ideas faded and turned into platitudes, and the grandest project of the Revolution—freedom, equality, fraternity—and the glory of the Napoleonic eagles constantly fed the hopes and dreams of many generations.

Consecutive plots, rebellions, and revolutions illustrated the immortality of Julien Sorel's grudge. Young people, sentenced to poverty, degraded and begrudged, chose the road of a revolution that was to change the course of the world. Sorel's contemporary Louis-Auguste Blanqui, a conspirator and revolutionary, admired by the people of the rebellion and hated by the people of success, rejected Cousin's theories and Guizot's practices. He declared that "a fight for life and death is on": the united aristocracy of the birth and money against the republicans and all the oppressed. A revolution is necessary as only it can "lighten up the horizon by cleansing the ground, and slowly take the curtains off, and open up the roads to a new order, . . . to a fundamental rebuilding of the society." "It is necessary to shatter the existing state apparatus," "dissolve the army and the judicial system," "recall all functionaries on the higher and medium level," "deport the clergy abroad," take over property of the Church, abolish the existing penal code and the judiciary, and replace the bourgeois dictatorship with the dictatorship of the armed people.[18]

That is the voice of Julien Sorel, who "refrained from the final shooting" by choosing the camp of the Revolution. It is hard not to relate to this boy of poor plebeian stock who did not want to accept his fate. The boy challenged the bad world in order to pursue his dream, until the very end. And what made that very end? The wise Stendhal found in Julien "a cold look showing a sovereign contempt." He also found "a still unformed longing for vengeance of the most atrocious order. Who would deny," stated Stendhal, "that such humiliating moments have given us the Robespierres of the world."[19]

Robespierre! The symbol of the Jacobin terror . . . When Danton was sentenced to the guillotine, a group of deputies demanded that he should be heard out. Robespierre rejected this demand with contempt, saying: "Who trembles now, is guilty."

Adam Sikora, author of a highly insightful essay on Blanqui, draws the following conclusions on the ideas of the great revolutionary: "Democratization of the civic life, expansion of political rights, election reform and universal suffrage—are all worthwhile things but only as means and not as goals. Therefore, the range of democratic reforms must be subject to the possibility of realizing the strategic goal, and to the consciousness of the people and their level of organization, as well as to the opposition strength of the enemies. Blanqui observed: 'To assume the very universal suffrage to be god the savior? That is a narrow strategy.' Moreover, it is a dangerous strategy because it is doomed to fail inevitably. After all, 'to ask the enslaved population about the opinion would mean to turn to their masters.' Hence, a conscious minority, the vanguard, must assume the responsibility and form the dictatorship which will function on behalf of the people, in accord with their vital interests, not always, however, asking the people for their opinion."[20]

Blanqui is said to have had "a heart and mind filled with the purest love of the revolution." They said the same about Robespierre—the Incorruptible. We shall always ask, however, how much of "the vague hope for the cruelest

vengeance" was in that "purest love." Sorel's grudge bred
that peculiar amalgamation that was the tragic experience
of all the revolutions of the twentieth century. A begrudged
rebellion and the need for vengeance changed a rebel into
an executioner—the fate of the heirs of Robespierre and
Danton, Julien Sorel and Auguste Blanqui, taught us that.
Therefore, we listen very carefully to the words of the rebels who wish to turn our whole world upside down. And
we closely watch their hands. We know all the sins and
villainies of this world of ours. Sometimes Stendhalian
fury grips us. We keep on trying to comprehend the mechanism of a creation of collective grudge which explodes in
a blind rebellion.

We do know that every revolution breeds beneficiaries and the disappointed. The beneficiaries will praise
the obvious benefits of the revolution: civic liberties and
representative government, open borders and the press
free of censorship, economic growth and free market,
new schools and universities, a flourishing banking
system and the goodies of the stock exchange, a con-
vertible currency and low inflation. The defeated and
the bitter, the excluded and the degraded will curse this
world and, perhaps, one more time will present their
bitter bill—made out to us, the beneficiaries.

VIII

Right in front of our eyes, we can see the marching parade of corrupt hypocrites, thick-necked racketeers, and venal deputies. Everyday villainy, pompous lies, and spiteful intrigue seem to be better than ever. Today, in our world, there exists no great idea of freedom, equality, and fraternity. There is no Napoleon among us and there is no promise of a great glory. We no longer believe in the man of the moment. We have been effectively cured of the belief in absolute justice. But that does not mean we accept the universal mean trickery and absolute injustice. After all, a Julien Sorel still endures the humiliations, a grudge is still growing in his heart, together with the envy and the hatred toward the world of the beneficiaries—to our world. Is he still repeating: *canaille, canaille, canaille*? Is he dreaming about the guillotine and retaliation? Or is he waiting for some sign of hope?

Perhaps, he waits for a Lafayette to show up, the one who did not steal and did not behead people; the one just a step away from ridicule but always far away from the wickedness?

That is the question . . .

The author of this book—a dissident and political prisoner during the period of Communist rule, and then, after 1989, editor-in-chief of the largest Polish newspaper, *Gazeta Wyborcza*—has been concerned with morality in politics from the very beginning of his writing career in the 1970s. The uniqueness of his perspective consists in combining his acute sense of political realism with a deep grounding in history and moral concerns. The texts in this collection reflect his latest thinking on these matters: Part One is devoted to the issues of political and historical fundamentalism and forgiveness; Part Two to detailed analysis, based on literary and historical sources, of post-revolutionary processes of social adaptation. Michnik uses the novels of Stendhal, one of his favorite writers, because they face turbulent and dark post-revolutionary times in all their moral complexity. Stendhal is faithful to political realities while holding to strong political convictions. This is also true of the author of this book.

The chapters of this book have been previously published in their original Polish in *Gazeta Wyborcza*. They are presented here in slightly different versions. Chapter 2 appeared in English in *International Journal of Politics, Culture, Society* (December 1, 2009), translated by Elzbieta Matynia. Chapter 1 was translated by Agnieszka Marczyk, and chapters 3–5 by Roman Czarny.

ONE  MORALITY IN POLITICS

1. A newspaper clip from 1970 quoted in Günter Grass, *My Century*, translated by Michael Henry Heim (New York: Harcourt Books, 1999), 185.

2. All of the quotations and reported words of German politicians come from Peter Merseburger's biography of Willy Brandt, as yet not translated into English, *Willy Brandt, 1913–1992: Visionär und Realist* (Stuttgart: DVA, 2003).

3. Grass, *My Century*, 185.

4. Ibid., 186–187.

5. Quoted in Gertjan Dijkink, *National Identity and Geopolitical Visions: Maps of Pride and Pain* (London: Routledge, 1996), 31.

6. Timothy Garton Ash, *In Europe's Name: Germany and the Divided Continent* (New York: Random House, 1993), 306.

THREE   THE ULTRAS OF MORAL REVOLUTION

1. G. W. F. Hegel, *The Philosophy of History*, translated by J. Sibree (New York: Dover Philosophical Classics, 1956), 450.

2. Hannah Arendt, *On Revolution* (New York: Viking Press, 1963), 89.

3. Ibid.

4. Ibid., 98.

5. "Notes rédigées par Robespierre à la veille du procès de Danton," in Albert Mathiez, *Études sur Robespierre* (Paris: Éditions sociales, 1973), 121–156.

6. Louis-Auguste Blanqui, *Notes Inédites sur Robespierre* (Paris, 1928); quoted after the Polish edition of the writings of Blanqui, *Wybór pism*, edited by Adam Sikora (Warsaw: Książka i Wiedza, 1975); all Blanqui quotations in this essay come from that edition.

7. Bill Schardt, "A Great and Virtuous Man? Joseph de Maistre (1753–1821)," *Newcastle Philosophy Society* (www.newphilsoc.org. uk/OldWeb1/Freedom/berlinday/a_great_and_virtuous_man. htm); Joseph de Maistre, *St. Petersburg Dialogues*, quoted in Isaiah Berlin, *The Crooked Timber of Humanity* (New York: Knopf, 1991), 116–117 (also in http://maistre.ath.cx:8000/st_petersburg.html).

8. Bolesław Miciński, "O nienawiści, okrucieństwie i abstrakcji," in *Pisma zebrane* (Warsaw: Więź, 2012), vol. 1.

9. Ibid.

10. Berlin, *The Crooked Timber*, 118–119.

11. Ibid., 119.

12. VeCheKa, known better as CheKa, stands for the All-Russian Extraordinary Commission.

13. Berlin, *The Crooked Timber*, 150.

14. Victor Hugo, *Les Misérables*, chapter 3, from "Requiescant," *The Literature Network* (www.online-literature.com/victor_hugo/les_miserables/170/).

15. G. Macaulay Trevelyan, *The English Revolution, 1688–1689* (Oxford: Oxford University Press, 1948), 9.

16. G. Macaulay Trevelyan, *History of England* (New York: Longmans, Green, 1926), 473.

17. Ibid., 474.

18. Ibid., 476.

19. Ibid.

FOUR  WILL YOU BE A TRUE SCOUNDREL?

The books by Stendhal this essay refers to are three novels, *Lucien Leuwen, The Red and the Black*, and *The Charterhouse of Parma*, as well as his fictionalized memoir *Memoirs of an Egotist*. Other books referred to are Jose Cabanis, *Charles X: The King of Ultras;* Sebastien-Roch-Nicolas Chamfort, *Maximes et Pensées;* Arnold Hauser, *The Social History of Art;* Paul Johnson, *The Birth of the Modern: World Society, 1815–1830;* Alfred de Vigny, *Servitude et Grandeur Militaires* and *Cinq Mars;* Dominique de Villepin, *One Hundred Days;* and Andrzej Zahorski, *France Between 1815–1849*.

1. Stendhal, *Lucien Leuwen* (Paris: Livres de Poche, 1960).

2. Georg Wilhelm Friedrich Hegel, *The Philosophy of History*, English translation (New York: Colonial Press, 1899), 449–453, quoted from "Liberty, Equality, Fraternity: Exploring the French Revolution," Roy Rosenzweig Center for History and New Media, George Mason University (http://chnm.gmu.edu/revolution/d/566/).

3. François-René de Chateaubriand, *Mémoires d'Outre-Tombe*, vol. 2, translated by A. S. Kline (Paris: Gallimard, 1951), 3–4,

quoted in "Napoleon and the Poets," by Jean-Baptiste Decherf, Association for the Study of Ethnicity and Nationalism conference, 2010, London School of Economics and Political Science (www.lse.ac.uk/researchAndExpertise/units/ASEN/Conference/PastConferences/2010/conferencepapers2010/Jean_Baptiste.pdf).

4. Stendhal, *Le Rouge et le Noir* (Paris: Garnier, 1960), 89.

5. Quoted in J. Pelczynski, *Hegel's Political Writings* (Oxford: Clarendon Press, 1964), 7.

6. Alfred de Musset, *Child of a Century*, e-text produced by David Widger, chapter 2, "Reflections" (www.fullbooks.com/Child-of-a-Century-entire1.html).

7. Alfred de Vigny, *Cinq Mars*, from *Project Gutenberg*, e-book produced by David Widger (www.gutenberg.org/files/3953/3953-h/3953-h.htm).

8. Alfred de Vigny, *Servitude et Grandeur Militaires*, from *Project Gutenberg*, e-book produced by Mireille Harmelin (www.gutenberg.org/cache/epub/18211/pg18211.html).

FIVE   CANAILLE, CANAILLE, CANAILLE!

The books by Stendhal this essay refers to are *The Red and the Black*, his *Korespondencje* (selected letters), his writings on Napoleon (*Napoléon: Vie de Napoléon*), and his fictionalized memoir *Memoirs of an Egotist*. Other books referred to are François de Chateaubriand, *The Memoirs;* Giuseppe Tomasi di Lampedusa, *On Stendhal;* and Jose Cabanis, *Charles X: The King of Ultras*.

1. Stendhal, *The Red and the Black* (Westminster, Md.: Random House, 2003), 292.

2. Ibid., 12.

3. Chateaubriand, *Mémoires d'Outre-Tombe*, translated by A. S. Kline, Book 13, *Poetry in Translation* (www.poetryintranslation.

com/PITBR/Chateaubriand/ChateaubriandMemoirsBookXIII. htm).

4. Stendhal, *Napoléon: Vie de Napoléon*, edited by H. Martineu (Paris: Le divan, 1930), from *Gallica: Bibliothèque Numérique*, Bibliothèque nationale de France (http://gallica.bnf.fr/ark:/12148/bpt-6k6923v/f2.image).

5. Giuseppe Tomasi di Lampedusa, *O Stendhalu*, translated by S. Kasprzysiak (Warsaw: Czytelnik, 2003), 37.

6. Stendhal, *The Red and the Black*, 279.

7. Ibid.

8. Ibid., 276.

9. Ibid., 283.

10. Ibid., 283.

11. Ibid., 282.

12. Ibid., 285.

13. Ibid., 132.

14. Ibid., 285.

15. Ibid., 284.

16. Ibid., 286–287.

17. Quoted after Adam Sikora, *Historia i prawdy wieczne* (Warsaw: PWN, 1977).

18. Louis-Auguste Blanqui, *Wybór pism*, edited by Adam Sikora (Warsaw: Książka i Wiedza, 1975).

19. Stendhal, *The Red and the Black*, 54.

20. Blanqui, *Wybór pism*.

# INDEX